Holy Ice

Holy Ice

Bridge to the Subconscious

by

Frank Dorland

Introduction by

Joseph Alioto, Ph.D.

1992
Galde Press, Inc.
P.O. Box 65611, St. Paul, Minnesota 55165, USA

First Edition

ISBN 1-880090-02-3

Photos by Frank Dorland

Dorland, Frank, 1914-
    Holy ice : bridge to the subconscious / by Frank Dorland :
    introduction by Joseph Alioto.
        p.   cm.
    Includes bibliographical references.
    ISBN 1-88090-02-3
    1. Quartz crystals--Miscellanea. 2. Crystal skulls.
    3. Occultism. 4. Parapsychology. I. Title.
    BF1442.C78D67 1992
    133--dc20   92-13885
                                                      CIP

 Printed on recycled paper

Galde Press, Inc.
P.O. Box 65611
St. Paul, Minnesota 55165

This book is lovingly dedicated to
Mabel, 1912-1991,
my co-worker and constant companion
for more than 53 years of work and joy.

About the Author

Frank Norton Dorland was born on October 11, 1914, in Peru, Nebraska, the third of six children. He had six years of college and university studies in San Diego and Los Angeles. On July 29, 1938, he married Mabel Vyvyan Jolliffe in her father's home in San Diego. During World War II, Frank worked as a preliminary design artist in the engineering division of Consolidated Aircraft at Lindbergh Field in San Diego. His work on design illustration, included the B-24 four engine bomber and the PBY-5 Catalina Patrol Seaplane as well as many others. After the war, Frank and Mabel designed and built their studio home on Hllside Drive overlooking the village of La Jolla. There, they pursued their joint careers as art conservators.

Frank researched and produced the first scientifically formulated artists' wax for painting and preserving art pieces, sculptures and archaeological artifcats. He supplied the wax originally to many artists and wood carvers, who dubbed it "Dorland's Wax." The name stuck and it is now nationally available in select art stores under the name Dorland's Wax Medium. It is manufactured by Siphon Arts in Richmond, California, with offices in San Rafael. In 1952, Frank was made member #122 of the International Institute for the Conservation of Museum Objects headquartered in London.

In 1959 the Dorlands moved from La Jolla to San Francisco. They purchased a three-story home at the end of the lagoon of the Palace of Fine Arts. In 1964, a full-size replica of a human skull carved out of quartz crystal was brought to the Dorlands from England. The subsequent studies of the crystal skull were so fascinating and time consuming that the Dorlands' art conservation practice gradually evolved into a new category: biocrystallography, the study of the interchange of energies between the human mind and electronic quartz crystal.

In 1970 the crystal skull was returned to Anna Mitchell-Hedges of Canada, who claims ownership of the artifact. From 1964 to 1990, Frank personally carved thousands of crystal working tools to supply demands in Bavaria, Australia, New Zealand, England, France, Italy, Canada and the United States.

Mabel Dorland died on March 4, 1991. Frank is semi-retired in his hillside studio home in San Luis Obispo County. He currently spends his time in further research on the hot wax painting technique as well as biocrystallography, studies on the human mind, dream control, and the development of creativity.

Frank Dorland appears in *Marquis Who's Who in the West*.

The Crystal

Pass not the shapeless lump of crystal by
Nor view its icy mass with careless eye.
Its royal value far exceeds
All the pearls the red seas bosom breeds.
This natural unformed stone without a grace
Midst rarest treasure
Holds the highest place.
                         —Claudianus (365-409 A.D.)

This poem by Claudianus reveals he was not thinking about the monetary sale value of crystals. He was hinting at mental and spiritual rewards to be gained. (Claudius Claudianus was a Latin epic poet who appeared in Rome during the reign of Arcadius and his brother Honorius. [378-408 A.D.]. Claudianus apparently was able to obtain the patronage of the Emperor Honorius. He was eventually honored by the placement of his statue in bronze in the Forum at Rome. Claudianus has been called "the last of the great Roman poets.")

CONTENTS

Introduction

The pages that lie ahead offer a fascinating account of the role of quartz crystals throughout history. The personal story of how the Dorlands came by the Mitchell-Hedges crystal skull and how their years of research with it changed their lives reads like an adventure novel. The legends and ancient cult practices relating to the use of quartz crystals are intriguing.

But perhaps the most exciting aspect of this book is about possibilities. That is, rather than simply being a compendium of anecdotes and stories about crystals, *Holy Ice* suggests some very interesting empirical hypotheses, especially to the scientifically curious—ideas that can be tried and tested if one had a mind to do so. While some readers will be content to accept or reject the information presented at face value, others might be inclined to say, "Let's try it and see what happens."

I encourage you to do so.

The greatest limitations to our understanding of the universe are self-imposed. Prior to 1492, people as a whole "knew" the earth was flat, but people like Christopher Columbus and Magellan said, "Let's go find out and see what happens."

In my own professional practice of medical and clinical psychology, I work daily with people to help them alleviate problems of chronic pain and stress-related disease caused by dysfunctional autonomic nervous systems. As a youngster, I was taught that internal organs such as the heart were "involuntary" and not under our conscious control. Rather, they were controlled by the autonomic nervous system (i.e., the "automatic" nervous system).

More recently, we have learned that, through the use of such techniques as biofeedback (the use of electronic equipment to feed back information to patients about their internal physiology—an electronic mirror, as it were), we can teach people to control their own autonomic nervous system, and thus control or eliminate such things as headaches, post-surgical pain, high blood pressure, etc.

Interestingly enough, this knowledge has existed for perhaps thousands of years in the context of certain yogic practices. However, it was not until some open-minded scientists could see the possibilities of combining this ancient wisdom with our state-of-the-art electronics that truly fruitful and helpful techniques could evolve. Biofeedback is but one example. Modern electronics, by the way, is based largely on the use of electronic crystals.

If you were to go to a culturally isolated village and describe to the inhabitants your knowledge of an invisible energy force that pervades all their surroundings, an energy force that would allow them to see and hear other people all over the world instantaneously, they might think you were either a great sorcerer or a great liar. Furthermore, if you were to suggest that they could capture these sounds and images through the use of a specially constructed box containing an assemblage of various pieces of metal and crystals, you would probably create quite a stir.

Well, of course, what has just been described is something we all take for granted in our daily lives—television. Yet, it was only a few short decades ago that this idea was relegated to the category of fantasy and science fiction.

What of the idea that you could store all the information from a library full of books on a handful of crystals and yet retrieve the information from one page of one of these books almost instantaneously? Well, isn't this just what our modern computers do for us? Based on a silicon crystal "chip," computers are rapidly changing our ability to control and process information. Of course, whether we will use this gift or power for our mutual growth and understanding or for our total destruction, only time will tell.

As Frank Dorland points out, the power of a quartz crystal lies not so much in the crystal itself as in the human being interacting with it. As you shall see in the pages ahead, man has been fascinated by the power of quartz crystals for many thousands of years. From a combination of fascination, curiosity and serendipity come the many reflections of what has been and what might be.

Although this book represents the culmination of many years of the author's life and work, it provides only a jumping off point for further study. An old Chinese adage states, "The journey of a thousand miles starts with one step."

My friends, your journey has already begun. Enjoy!

—Joseph T. Alioto, Ph.D.
San Luis Obispo, California

Preface

Holy Ice is the story of quartz crystal, the miracle ingredient in the "New" Age. The average person thinks of quartz as an almost worthless mineral found in abundance everywhere. Its chemical name is silicon dioxide, which truly is an ordinary material—it exists in about 80 per cent of the earth's crust.

But one valuable type of silicon dioxide is not common. Found in a form sometimes known as rock crystal, in ancient days this pure, clear, transparent quartz was once called "holy ice."

This name came from the belief that solid crystal was originally holy water that God poured out of heaven for the benefit of mankind. As the water fell through the frigid air of outer space, it became frozen into solid ice. Guardian angels, witnessing God's gift, feared that the frozen holy water would melt and sink into the earth. They promptly petrified the water so it would forever remain solid and be available to mankind as a permanent blessing—a solid link with heaven. Since crystal does not oxidize, change with age or decay, it is a truly permanent gemstone.

Quartz crystal is the emerging symbol for the next great period of history—the Age of Aquarius. One might imagine that the portrayal of the statuesque Aquarian water bearer pouring sacred water out of an ever-flowing jug is a symbol of the energy that continuously flows from electronic crystals.

In the Aquarian Age, also touted as the age of communications, this magical crystal and the knowledge derived from its use is destined to be the electronic catalyst that allows blessings in abundance for the human race to come within practical reach.

From the simplest five-watt radio gear to the most elaborate television network; from the sophisticated electronic miracles in medicine and healing to the nourishment and culture of the human mind in all its creative powers, the electronic crystals are truly a Godsend of the highest magnitude. They can aid, reflect and amplify the greatest dreams of the human race. A human being is a living, walking liquid crystal of amazing potential.

—Frank Dorland

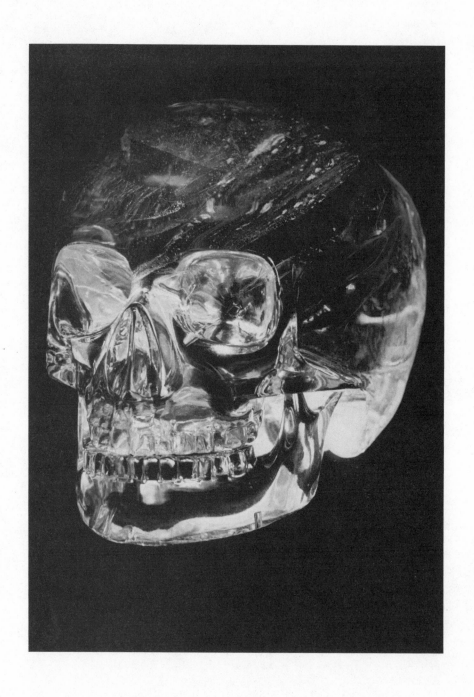

The Crystal Skull
A Personal History

In the 1950s, my wife Mabel and I first heard about an archaeological curiosity called the Mitchell-Hedges crystal skull, then
residing at Farley Castle in England.

Since we were an art conservation team specializing in research
on religious art objects, the news of the existence of the skull was of
great interest to us. We heard that the skull had been at the British
Museum for at least a year for examination, but we felt that the
results of their investigations were inconclusive.

The British Museum Report
There was a scholarly report comparing the Mitchell-Hedges
skull to the British Museum crystal skull. It was published in the
July 1936 issue of *Man*, which was a monthly publication of anthro-
pological sciences issued under the direction of the Royal Anthro-
pological Institute of Great Britain and Ireland. (Most large universities should have a copy in their library.)

Following is a summary of this document prepared by
anthropologist Dr. G. M. Morant, Adrian Digby and J. J. Braun-
holtz of the British Museum in London:

Dr. Morant writes that there are only two known authentic

life-size representations of the human skull carved in solid rock crystal. One was in the British Museum and the other was in the hands of a Mr. Sydney Burney. (The Sydney Burney skull and the Mitchell-Hedges skull are one and the same. In the British Museum paper of 1936 it was called the Burney skull.)

Dr. Morant states that both skulls were remarkably similar in size and shape. Furthermore, it was curious that neither of them had suture marks normally found on all human skulls. Using very technical terms, Dr. Morant felt that both skulls showed suggestions of "femaleness."

It was noted that the only marked difference between the two skulls was that the British Museum specimen was in one solid piece, but the Burney skull had a removable jawbone with teeth. It was further declared that the British skull was a crude representation, while the Burney skull was far more successful in being anatomically accurate and lifelike. Dr. Morant concludes that the two skulls obviously could not be of independent origin because of their remarkable similarities of size, shape and technical measurement. Both had to be representations of the same human skull. This original skull used as a model did not have the usual European cranium. However, it easily could have been of Native-American extraction.

Digby went on to write that there was no trace of identifiable tool marks on either skull. In 1965, however, I found and identified parallel repeating scratches made by a rotary tool device. These tool marks were found only on the face of the teeth in the removable jaw of the Mitchell-Hedges skull.

At that time, Digby believed that both skulls might have been Mexican in origin. He went on to say that the two skulls may somehow be related but it would be rash to conclude that they were modeled from the same human skull. He expressly noted the height of the British skull was greater than that of the Burney skull, and he believed it would be unwise to assume any definite conclusions on either skull.

I would like to point out that, if the British skull were taken to a skilled lapidary and had the jaw piece cut loose, the loss of material from the saw cut, the sanding, polishing and finishing of the jawbone would account for a substantial loss of rock crystal. After completion of this procedure, the height of the two skulls would be practically identical.

H. J. Braunholtz of the British Museum concludes the paper

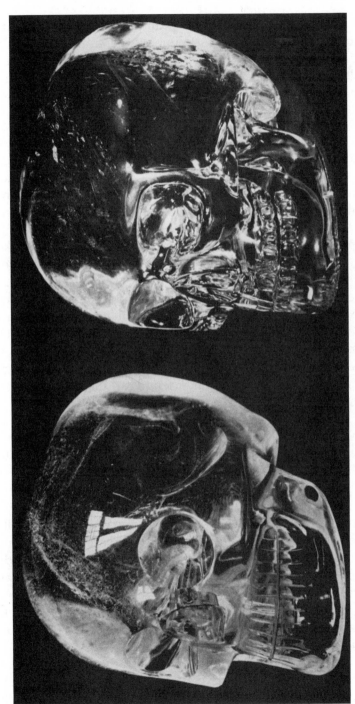

Comparison of British Skull and Mitchell-Hedges Skull

by affirming that the British skull is entirely in line with other known, authentic Aztec specimens, therefore it might be quite acceptable as an example of pre-Columbian Aztec sculpture. Braun-holtz further stated that the Burney skull was so realistic that it had the character of an anatomical model in a scientific age.

An Unreported Prism

The report in the *Man* journal never mentioned the existence of a most extraordinary flat prism surface carved in the roof of the mouth in the Mitchell-Hedges skull. This would be a major, time-consuming lapidary feat. All the work would be hidden from nor-mal sight unless the skull was turned upside down. The prism was carefully positioned to reflect light from below (a temple fire per-haps?) which would then be plainly visible in both eye sockets.

The report also ignores two small drilled holes, one on the right and one on the left side in the lower mastoid process area. These two small holes could act as support-bearing surfaces. This means that the crystal skull could be balanced upright resting on two slender pins inserted in the two holes, thus allowing the skull to be viewed as a moving, nodding oracle if its owners so wished. These two, tiny holes indicate a carefully and precisely engineered scheme of very high intelligence and not the result of accident or coincidence.

These facts among others are why Mabel and I were positive the crystal skull had to be much more important than the British Museum seemed to believe. It seemed to represent substantially rich material dealing with spiritual beliefs reaching far into the very soul of mankind.

Most ancient civilizations had great respect for the skull, bor-dering on worship, because it is the container of the intellect, the personality, the being and the soul of a human being during his or her existence on this physical plane. The skull, or head, is the important portion, and the body is merely a mechanism attached to it to serve its needs.

In spite of many movies, television shows, comic books, pop-ular literature and medicine bottles, the skull is a symbol of death *only to the uninitiated.*

Almost everyone who hears about the crystal skull seems to experience a strong reaction. Mabel and I were fascinated because of our special interest in religious art. At that time, we discussed the skull with members of the academic and scientific community and were dismayed at their attitude. Almost unanimously, they believed the skull to be a hoax.

As professional art conservators, we could not agree because we knew that fake artworks are produced to meet market demands. The motive is money. To carve a masterful rendition of a full-size human skull out of quartz crystal would be so expensive to produce that it would utterly fail to be profitable.

A crude, hastily made rendition *could* be profitable. However, the demand would need to be commercially promoted over a period of time to be successful.

Also, the crystal skull did not fit in with any accepted normal classification. It is well known that art dealers are not keen on odd-ball items that raise a lot of questions; their money is more easily made on standard goods that are in demand and easily salable. If a forger wanted to sell something to this market, he would not produce such an unusual item.

AUTHENTICATION

A good art investigator always plays a game called "the devil's disciple," in which he or she searches for any possible discrepancies in an object being studied. This is the practical approach; if one can find fault with something, another "expert" could do likewise. When serious errors cannot be found, the object in question is assumed to be possibly authentic and of true value. Only after all efforts to discredit an object have failed is it considered provident to spend research time to discover the true facts concerning it. Mabel and I deduced that the skull could be very important; however, the big question remained. What was it and what was its purpose?

This world-famous artifact was known as the Mitchell-Hedges crystal skull, named after the English explorer and adventurer, F. A. Mitchell-Hedges. He refused to divulge where or how he got the skull, saying only that he had a very good reason not to tell. He felt the skull could be an evil thing in the wrong hands and called it "The Skull of Doom." The British press loved this title; to this day, it is sometimes referred to by that name.[1]

THE KEEPER OF THE CRYSTAL SKULL

After Mitchell-Hedges' death, the skull was claimed by his adopted daughter, Anna, known to her friends as "Sammy." She was Mitchell-Hedges's almost lifelong confidante and companion and accompanied him on some of his exploring adventures into the wilds of Africa and America. Sammy stated that she had personally discovered the skull when probing through the ruins of the ancient city of Lubaantun in British Honduras (now Belize).

"It's mine," she said. "It belongs to me."

The British Museum also has its crystal skull, and it was reported that they cast sideways glances at the Mitchell-Hedges skull, perhaps because, at that time, only two full-size crystal skulls were known to exist—the British Museum skull, which was simply labeled pre-Columbian, and the Mitchell-Hedges crystal skull, which resided at Farley Castle near Reading in Berkshire, England, along with Mitchell-Hedges and Sammy.

Sammy said that Burney had the skull as collateral for a loan. Whisperings from the museum, however, told me it was Burney who owned the skull. Unable to find a buyer, he sold it for a relatively small price to Mitchell-Hedges—who was an antique dealer, among other things. Here are more mysteries, but the skull itself is remarkable and outstanding. It is human beings who have clouded it.

Our story begins when we first met Sammy and her extraordinary treasure in New York City. She had brought the skull with her from England on a business trip to New York during the 1964-1965 World's Fair.

FROM NEW YORK TO SAN FRANCISCO AND BEYOND

It was a crisp fall day in New York when we first met Sammy. We liked her immediately. Her eyes mirrored a warm, generous personality bubbling over with enthusiasm. She stepped into our taxi carrying her purse under one arm and clutching a large, almost square black box with the other. Our destination was the Heye Foundation, better known as the Museum of the American Indian. Sammy wished to pay her respects to the director and to see if some of the many artifacts given to the museum by her father were on display.

F. A. Mitchell-Hedges

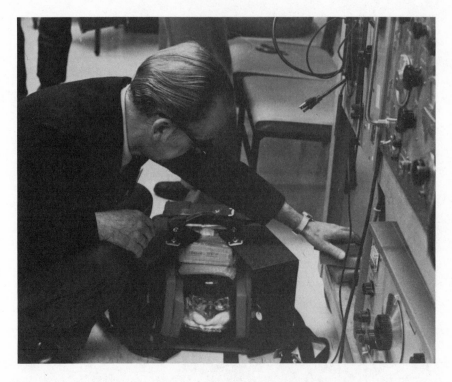

Frank Dorland with Crystal Skull in Carrying Case

As the taxi threaded its way through traffic, I studied the unusual black box, which by this time was on my lap. It was quite heavy and big enough to hold a bowling ball. Double doors that locked in the middle in front were hinged where the sides met the back. This meant that the front and sides could swing wide open in one unit, something like a clam shell, to display the contents. The box was bound with four stout, black-cloth belts. Two were wrapped around the box side by side horizontally and two were wrapped vertically. Obviously, this box couldn't open accidentally.

We arrived at the museum and I dismissed the taxi; I had no idea how long we might be there. The director was expecting us, and we were taken directly to his office. The black box was growing heavier with every step. I was happy to place it on a table when the door shut behind us.

The director appeared within moments of our arrival, and, after opening introductions and polite talk, Sammy announced

Anna Mitchell-Hedges

that she had brought the crystal skull with her. After removing the four black belts, she pushed the two doors outward and there it sat, glistening and glorious, a fabulous treasure to see. The deep icy eyes staring out at us had a hypnotic influence—at least on me.

"This skull is magical," I murmured half aloud, and was startled to hear the director comment:

"Yes, it is," he said.

We then spent several hours at the museum and saw many objects that had been collected by F. A. Mitchell-Hedges. Late in the day, we finally headed back toward our hotel.

We saw Sammy several more times in New York City before our last meeting there, which was in the office of the legal counsel for the World's Fair police. We were there to pick up a small but very valuable religious painting that had been on display at the fair. Known as the "Black Virgin of Kazan," this Russian icon depicts the classic mother and child and is covered with a hammered gold *riza* (garment) encrusted with more than a thousand precious gems. It depicts the hope and the salvation of the Mysterious Mother who nourishes and strengthens and provides for all who come to her.

This famed icon is illustrated on page 58 of the hardcover edition of the *1964-1965 New York World's Fair Souvenir Book,* opposite the *Pieta* of Michelangelo. Our job was to take the icon back to San Francisco for safekeeping.

The icon had been in our care since March 1, 1962, and we were displaying it at the fair in an attempt to restore it to the Russian church where it rightfully belonged. Previously it had mysteriously vanished from its home, the Kazan Cathedral on Red Square in Moscow during the 1917 Bolshevik Revolution. An analysis of the pigments used in the icon indicated a process used before the 14th century. This served to confirm that it was the one taken from Kazan Cathedral.

According to legend, the icon has amazing powers. It is said to have driven invading Poles from the Kremlin and to have caused Napoleon to leave Moscow—and to be responsible for the end of the communist regime. After Kazan Cathedral was demolished by the Bolsheviks, no one could build any secular building on that site; no construction would stand there. The icon had been smuggled out of country at the time of the revolution and had been hidden in

Black Virgin of Kazan and Mitchell-Hedges Crystal Skull

Poland until 1935. Mitchell-Hedges purchased it in 1953.

Sammy arrived at the office about the same time we did, once more carrying the black box. Just before we entered the inner offices where the officers and the attorneys were waiting, she told us that we were to take the crystal skull to San Francisco with us. We three then went to the inner room where Mabel and I completed the formalities of transferring physical possession of the icon from the fair into our hands. It took quite a while, since the attorneys apparently wanted everything to be very thorough and binding.

The irreplaceable icon was valued so highly that we felt comfortably relieved when an armored limousine with guard was assigned to provide our transportation when we left. In a few hours, we were at the Kennedy International Airport where Mabel and I, carrying the skull in its black box and the encased icon inside a tweed canvas tote sack, were escorted aboard the airplane by the guard. We waved goodbye to Sammy just as we entered the plane. The guard insisted on staying with us until we were seated.

In a matter of moments we were speeding down the runway, and then liftoff, a smooth climb and a beeline straight for home. The countryside far below slid silently by, outlined in complex patterns of squares and rectangles. The seat directly across the aisle was unoccupied, so I strapped the black box in the seat with the skull facing forward. I felt it would be more secure there than on the floor at my feet.

The stewardess was greatly intrigued by this and, although she did not say anything to us, she eyed the black box suspiciously all the way across the United States.

The landing at San Francisco was smooth as satin, and shortly after the valet service had our station wagon at the curb. We loaded the luggage, cushioned and covered the painting and the black box in fire-resistant blankets always kept in the back of the wagon and nosed out onto the highway.

Soon we were driving across the Golden Gate Bridge toward our studio in Marin County. Mabel mentioned that we should find a very safe place to keep these two extraordinarily valuable objects. Although our home and studio had an elaborate three-way crime and fire detection system, it would have been foolhardy to leave these treasures there except during times of treatment and research.

Within a few days, we discovered that the Mill Valley branch of the Bank of America had one very large vault in their safe-deposit section. The vault had been used in the Gold Rush days to store gold bullion and silver dollars, but they had little use for it in 1964. We were welcome to rent it by the year for a modest sum, so we stored them together: the black box containing the skull and the religious painting. There was still plenty of room left in the vault. We were elated with our good fortune—the bank was less than a 10-minute drive from our studio home on the mountainside above it. Little did we realize how much help this arrangement would be. We expected perhaps a year of studies, but our estimate grew into more than six years of intensive research and care— along with some unexpected intrigues and dangers.

Exterior of Dorland's Marin County Art Conservation Studio

Interior of Art Conservation Studio

STRANGE PHENOMENA

Soon, peculiar things started to occur whenever the skull was out of the vault. We noticed that, when we were making notes or were very quiet, we could hear soft voices and music. Sometimes there was an odor—an elusive, sweet-sour, wet fragrance that reminded me of apple blossoms and vinegar mixed with the unmistakable smell of an icy mountain stream. If we put our hands close to the skull, we could feel a tingling like an electrical current, and there were other times when we clearly saw shapes and shadows moving about inside it.

Here was an inanimate object sitting on a research desk in our studio—singing to us, speaking to us, filling the air with a fleeting sweet-sour perfume and tingling our fingers with electrical energy. Not only that, but we were starting to see things. I was puzzled and becoming a little edgy.

One night, it grew too late to take the skull back to the vault. Because of the crisp, cold weather outside, we built a fire in our Norwegian stove in the far corner across the room from the couch. In front of the couch, we had a low, onyx-top coffee table. To keep the skull in plain view, we put it on the coffee table. After dinner, I sat down on the couch and glanced at the fire across the room. I looked down at the skull directly in front of me and was startled to see a dancing fire in each eye socket. The eyes were alive with flames.

As soon as I regained my composure, I shouted for Mabel to come running. Together, we watched and pondered the extremely hypnotic display. I saw immediately, as did Mabel, that it displayed a feat of scientific optical achievement supposedly unknown to ancient races. With a few additional experiments, we found that the skull was *intentionally* carved to perform a whole series of optical illusions by reflecting the lights from nearby fires in various locations.

After a few more weeks of studies, we decided that, since the skull was producing sounds, odors, visions, and touch sensations, we needed to apply some strict rules in the future to remove any doubts about the accuracy of our observations. Both of us by this time had observed little episodes visible inside the skull—snatches of scenes of strange places and events. We wondered if anyone would believe this.

When I looked at the skull, it seemed to turn cloudy then

Oakland Natural History Museum Crystal Ball

clear. If I kept gazing at it, scenes would often appear with people, buildings, animals, meadows, trails and mountains.

Mabel also saw many visions within the skull. When we compared our happenings we found that neither of us experienced the same or even similar scenarios.

We decided we must completely eliminate any mind-altering substances from our lives. No more cocktails, no more coffee or tea or any item that could possibly be suspect in any way. The elimination of alcohol was an easy safeguard to guarantee the absence of such future questions as, "How many cocktails did you have before you saw the pictures in the skull?" We also decided that we would look for a standard crystal to compare with the skull during research studies, and we could think of no better standard than a large crystal ball.

The next day, after returning the skull to its bank vault for safety, we started looking for a crystal ball to purchase. We discovered a most amazing thing. There were literally thousands of crystal balls available, but all of them were imitation. That is, they were made of either lead crystal, which is glass with a high lead content, or they were plastic or plain old-fashioned glass. We could not find one single authentic quartz crystal ball to buy.

We eventually found a genuine crystal ball in the natural history department of the Oakland Museum across the Bay, but of course it was not for sale. The museum had two balls in their collection from the Gold Rush era. In those days, several Chinese craftsmen had carved crystal balls in San Francisco. The raw crystal was a by-product, blasted out of the mountains when the Chinese laborers were building the railroads. One of the balls at the museum was ideal because it had inclusions in the crystal almost identical to those in the skull.

The museum authorities were pleased to loan us the ball for our research. We had their crystal ball for several years sitting side by side with the crystal skull as a comparative standard. We found that the crystal ball performed in the same way as the skull. Though not quite as potent a force and not quite as large, the ball repeated the same sort of phenomena—patterns of sounds, odors, a sense of touch and visions.

In time, after an evaluation of our findings, we came to the conclusion that there were sufficient clues to postulate that electronic quartz crystal broadcasts energies on a wavelength compatible with and receivable by body cells and the subconscious and conscious mind. We concluded that the skull shape or form was not important in producing the phenomena. The important thing was that the skull was a large chunk of active electronic quartz crystal. The material itself was the cause!

At this same time we had another interesting experience. We had just purchased a new Rogers electronic organ and had it delivered and installed. When we turned it on, strange human voices came out of the speaker cabinets. In trouble-shooting this difficulty, we discovered that the voices originated from the nearby RCA overseas communication station. The organ, by a strange electronic phenomenon, received and amplified telephone conversations between San Francisco, Honolulu and Japan.

We reported this to the Federal Communication Commission. They sent two men up to the mountainside who showed us how we could apply some shielding and a filter to eliminate the voice interference. This experience made us realize that, if our organ received unintended, stray radio messages from space, perhaps the human mind could receive a few natural wavelength signals from electronic quartz. The phenomenon doesn't seem so strange when we compare these two experiences.

The pace of our research increased, and we discovered there were more things going on in the invisible world that surrounded us than we had ever imagined. As an example, if you were to stretch a string from one side of a room to the other and divide that string into known wavelengths, you would find that the section capable of being sensed by the five senses of human beings is infinitesimally minute.

Human detection capabilities in the average person are currently estimated to be less than two per cent of the known wavelength spectrum. This means that most of us are not aware of 98 per cent of the events that surround us at all times.

THE SKULL AT HEWLETT-PACKARD

Another remarkably unusual feature of the skull is its removable jawbone. If the jawbone had originally been attached and part of the skull and then later cut loose, it would be of major importance. To cut the jawbone loose from the skull and carve it to shape would be many times more difficult than merely carving a separate jawbone from another chunk of crystal.

Not only would it have been extremely difficult and hazardous to cut the jawbone from the skull, but also there was the implication that the skull was a major religious object requiring the utmost care, regardless of time or cost. Our research had to determine whether the jaw piece was originally a part of the solid block of crystal that the skull was carved from.

A major electronics company of international reputation, Hewlett-Packard, was located just south of San Francisco in the famous Silicon Valley. I arranged to visit them, and, in November 1970, I took the skull to their facilities in Santa Clara. I showed them the crystal skull and described the help I needed from them. News of a human skull carved out of crystal ran through the entire plant in less than an hour. It was suggested I come back another day and speak to all the employees in the main auditorium. They

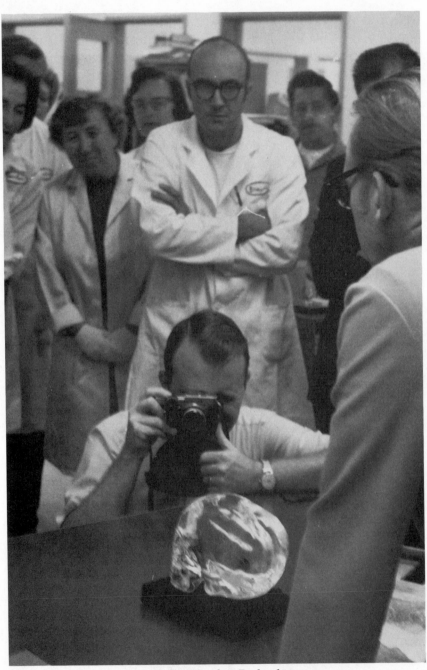

Staff at Hewlett-Packard
(Frank Dorland with back to camera)

Skull on Optical Bench
The skull is on a rotating pad between two polarized screens,
one to polarize the light source and the other for viewing and calibration.

Skull Submerged in Tank of Benzyl Alcohol
for Viewing with Polarized Light and Screen

promised they would then do a complete diagnostic examination.

I returned to Hewlett-Packard at the appointed time with the skull. The auditorium was packed. I spoke and projected my set of color slides of the inside and outside of the skull and did my best to explain about the skull: where it came from, what it was and why it was so important.

After lunch we met in the science laboratory for the examination. The skull was immersed in a tank of benzyl alcohol which closely matches the refractive index of quartz crystal. The tank had glass sides to allow light projection and viewing. The skull was barely visible, because when crystal is immersed in a matching refractive liquid it tends to become invisible. Polarized light was then projected through the tank and skull, and viewing was done through a polarized screen. We could easily see wavy stress lines throughout the face of the skull and the jawbone. The wavy lines reminded me of moiré patterns.

The lines went from the skull to the jaw piece in a perfect continuation of pattern without the slightest flaw or mismatch. There was no possible doubt. The jaw piece was once an integral part of the skull and was later cut loose so it could be a separate piece. I will forever be grateful to the people at Hewlett-Packard for their friendly help.

VISITORS

While we were quietly working with the crystal skull on the California mountainside, some newspapers, magazines, radio and television coverage used small items about the skull every now and then. The word spread. The crystal skull seemed to be working its own kind of magic to let people know where it was and what was happening.

The skull made an enormous impression on the general public, but almost everybody had misconceptions about it. Mabel and I were barraged with ideas about how to put the skull to work. Unfortunately, almost every one of these plans was unrealistic or downright weird.

We were approached in San Francisco by a group of holographic light entrepreneurs who had "a great idea to set San Francisco on its ear." They planned to holographically project and enlarge the skull to giant proportions and have it appear as if it were suspended in midair high above the heads of the parishoners in Grace Cathedral on Nob Hill. They thought about a week to 10 days would be sufficient to make an impression. Why they imagined Bishop Pike would permit such a display is an unsolved mystery.

We were then contacted by a traveling circus troop that desperately wanted a plastic copy of the skull to be the star of the side show. The circus officials promised me that the skull would be treated with the utmost possible respect. It would be ceremoniously carried on a litter embellished with gold filigree. The litter would be carried by four muscular men dressed in golden loincloths. In attendance would be 12 dancing girls. "We will go to all extremes to get 12 of the hottest kootch dancers in America," they told me.

These anecdotes are included simply to illustrate some of the things people thought the skull would be good for. They were sincere, and they were proud of their ingenious ideas. Unfortunately, their creativity was misplaced.

Soon a small but steady stream of visitors from many countries came calling. In a short time, we became quite adept at fending off the merely curious and the potentially dangerous ones, but there were many bona fide seekers; these we could not refuse.

Mabel played hostess to literally dozens of searchers. The skull attracted psychologists, shamans, psychiatrists, medicine men, university professors, witch doctors, voodoo priests, and many others. Soon we discovered we could clearly detect the honest seekers. The real searchers were always low key but positive and obviously in full command at all times. They were well mannered, well bred, well educated, and well dressed.

It was a fascinating experience to sit with the crystal skull and talk with a Mongolian medicine man dressed in a Brooks Brothers suit, who spoke excellent English and held graduate and post-graduate degrees from several universities here and abroad. We are most grateful for the very valuable help given us by sincere and intelligent visitors. Their information was freely given and in almost all cases no conditions were demanded or restrictions asked.

About this time a writer and newspaper editor named Sibley Morrill became very interested in the crystal skull. Sibley became a frequent visitor at our home. He asked if he could bring an acquaintance who was an expert in magical practices to see the skull, and I said yes.

The next afternoon Sibley was at the door with Anton LaVey. Sibley said it should be very interesting to hear the opinion of a "real expert," and that LaVey could certainly qualify.

After entering the house, LaVey saw the organ in the living room. Immediately drawn to it, he sat down and played. His abilities as an accomplished keyboard artist were obvious. We soon found out that he had worked as an organist in a bar; before that he had been a lion tamer in a carnival. All that was before he became the head of the Church of Satan.

After he played several pieces on the organ, LaVey spent the rest of the afternoon looking at the skull and talking about it, giving his opinions. He was entranced by it and stayed quite late. He claimed the skull was always meant to be used for evil purposes, that it was an energy source designed to give strength to the powers of darkness. He wasn't interested in hearing other facts about the skull. I don't suppose Satanists ever are. Mr. LaVey was a powerful man, intelligent and likable. Why he chose to promote the powers of darkness I shall never understand.

Since our guest stayed too late for us to get the skull back into the bank vault, we had to keep it at home overnight. As the evening hours passed, we heard more and more strange sounds.

We went to bed around 11:30 P.M. At midnight, the volume of strange sounds increased tremendously. There was a swell of harmonic chanting and the babble of many voices. Moanings like the wind in the gables were evident, yet the night was still with no wind. We heard sharp clicking noises like several Ping-Pong balls bouncing in a nearby room. There were repeated sounds of a large beast that would pad up and down the hallway and stairs.

These sounds were very much like those made by our three cats when they raced up and down the hallway and stairs. The cats weighed seven to ten pounds each. However, this noise sounded like a 190-pound animal running around in the darkness.

Because of our work in art conservation, which involved being responsible for other people's property, our studio and home were very secure against any unwanted visitors. It was impossible for anything or anyone to enter the house without tripping the three-way alarms. The cats were securely locked away in their own area, a separate room. The elaborate alarm system did not go off because

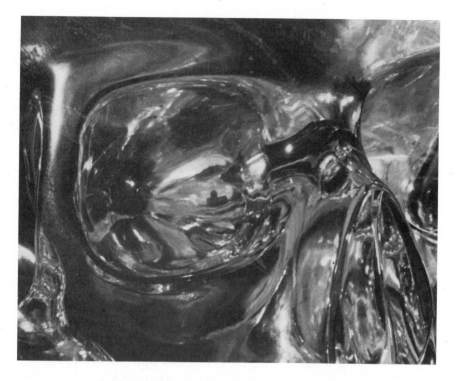

Enlargement of Right Eye Socket of Crystal Skull

no doors or windows had been opened.

The noises continued throughout most of the night, and in the morning we found that physical objects had been moved. We classified the night's activities as poltergeist phenomena caused by a strong conflict of energies between the normal oscillations of the skull and those of Anton LaVey.

In midmorning, we took the skull back to the bank vault. The incident was the first and last that we personally experienced of a disturbing type of activity associated with the skull.

When we allowed visitors to view the skull we were careful to stay close by to enforce our rule that no one would be allowed to touch or handle the skull. We had to be alert at all times, because some viewers were susceptible to entering a trance or semi-trance state when looking at the skull. We discovered that the most rapid mental changes occurred when someone stared directly into the eye sockets.

We later discovered the importance of the inside/outside

curve of the eye socket.

We know that electronic waves are broadcast easier from a crystal that has rounded, polished surfaces rather than flat planes.

The reverse curve in the eye socket, or like the letter "S" seems to amplify the broadcasting power. Perhaps it's some kind of energy producer that operates much the same way as cracking a whip.

One example of intense visual interaction happened when a newspaper editor, a working colleague of Sibley Morrill, was allowed to closely examine the skull at his own request. He was quite defensive and obviously had intentions of writing some sort of an exposé. Suddenly, the room was deadly silent. The editor was staring directly into the eye sockets of the skull and appeared as though he were in a trance. In a few moments, he proved it as he began softly swearing and muttering to himself in an unintelligible jargon.

I immediately began interfering with his mental state by moving around and asking direct questions. These distractions disrupted his trance. With a puzzled look on his face, he asked me why I had turned on the flashing lights that had blinded and confused him. In 15 minutes or so he was back to normal, and before he left he denied to me and himself that anything unusual had occurred.

Another curious example happened one evening in 1972 when a local public relations man and author named Richard Garvin arrived at our home. He needed additional information for a new book he was writing entitled *The Crystal Skull*. The book was published by Doubleday in 1973, with Simon & Schuster's paperback edition following in 1974. The Japanese edition was printed in 1975.

After a short discussion of some corrections and additions to the book, Garvin sat quietly staring at the skull.

He then spoke. "I wonder what you really are. I wonder what you mean," he pondered.

He then became quite agitated and blurted out, "I think it's trying to talk. Look at it! It's trying to tell me something, but it's bleeding. It's bleeding at the mouth!"

We calmed Mr. Garvin the best we could, and he soon returned to normal.

I thought that this experience with Garvin and the skull was a most interesting event because the upper front teeth of the crystal skull are actually chipped as a result of some long-past accident.

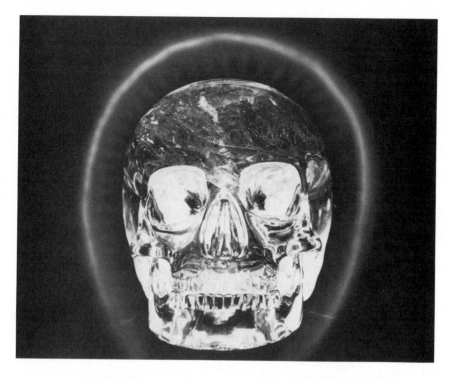

Recreated Aura Observed Around Skull in Meditation

Did this cause Garvin to have such a strange reaction? He was very upset because he believed the skull was trying to answer him but could not because it was injured.

Garvin had several trance or semi-trance experiences that I observed carefully during our association. Unfortunately, he never seemed to remember any of them and later denied they had ever happened. He stated in radio and television appearances that he had never personally seen anything out of the ordinary when he saw the skull. In the conclusion of his book, *The Crystal Skull,* he wrote, "I have never been able to witness any of these phenomena."

Our research indicates that this kind of memory lapse is not uncommon. One researcher told me that he believed the experience was similar to dreams that dissolve and vanish into nothingness when we awaken to our five-sense world in the morning. In like manner, many psychics have said they never remember anything they say or do while in trance. They seemingly live in two worlds with twin existences that never meet.

On the other hand, I do know certain excellent psychics who seem to be fully aware in either trance or normal consciousness. Their memory is clear and accurate for either mental state.

Numerous psychics clamored for a personal viewing of the skull. We were told by many that the skull was undoubtedly a storehouse of great secrets that could only be brought out in privacy because "the world is not yet ready to receive such astounding truths." In response to a number of fascinating proposals, we selected several dozen individuals over a period of time to sit in front of the skull and "do their thing."

We observed each session with anticipation, but we eventually became discouraged because no common trend or mutually compatible message emerged. These sessions were consistent only in their inconsistencies.

What we then realized was that each psychic was being stimulated by the feedback—crystal-amplified energies they originally put out from their own subconscious and conscious minds. Instead of psychic readings about the crystal skull and its secrets, we were witnessing a sort of spontaneous do-it-yourself personal psychoanalysis. None of the psychics ever seemed to realize they were dredging up their own personal loves, hates and fears from their inner depths.

In trying to correct this deviation from our goal, we started a series of meditation exercises with the skull. What soon became apparent was that merely meditating in the presence of the skull did not insure success. We eventually discovered that it was necessary to prepare for each meditation. The best preparation consisted of writing down simple, short questions that we wanted answered. We had to prepare a sensible and logical format to follow if we were to get sensible and logical answers.

Again, we were shown that clarity and control of the human mind is of vital importance in all aspects of crystal usage. The electronic quartz crystal is a miraculous device—the world's first solid-state tool—but the human mind must control the crystal. The mind is the power supply; the crystal is the reflecting amplifier.

THE NEW PROFESSION: BIOCRYSTALLOGRAPHY

We continued our studies in the paranormal. The days, weeks and months slipped steadily past. As we became absorbed with our studies about crystals, our activities in art conservation were suffering from neglect. We talked for many hours about this, and finally decided to cut our ties with the art field.

This was a difficult decision to make, because we had built up the finest art conservation laboratory on the West Coast. We were both members in good standing of the International Institute for Conservation in London, and we had collected a large library of reference materials. Our reputation and our contacts brought us a steady business, but we also loved our work with the skull.

The series of new discoveries concerning electronic crystals appealed to both of us, so we succumbed to the lure of a future in this new science—biocrystallography, which loosely means the interchange of energies between the human mind and the quartz crystal.

Nearly two years were necessary to phase out all of the art activities. We gradually exchanged the specialized equipment useful only to treat art objects into other specialized equipment used to study, cut, carve and work with quartz crystals. Many of our art reference materials were donated to the Mill Valley Public Library.

By this time, the need to make some scientific models of the skull to facilitate more intensive studies became obvious. We made "glove molds" of the skull and the separate jaw piece which allowed us to reproduce the skull in polyester plastic. We made dozens of accurate scientific copies. These copies were sliced into sections, giving us more precise measurements of the configuration and mass of the skull.

Several full copies were completed for the purpose of proving or disproving a theory that the skull was used as a mechanized talking oracle in the jungle temples of British Honduras. Eventually, the model skull was mounted on a stand to accommodate two mysterious bearing-like holes found in the base of the crystal skull. It was discovered that the skull balanced perfectly when two tiny support rods entered these two holes. This seemed to indicate that the skull was once mounted on a supporting stand that held the skull in an upright, balanced position. By means of push rods or strings, the skull could easily be manipulated like a puppet. The jaw floated freely to move up and down as if speaking, and the skull would nod and shake in a convincing manner.

With the addition of altar fires to the sides, behind and below the skull inside a hollow stone altar, various mood-enhancing light-

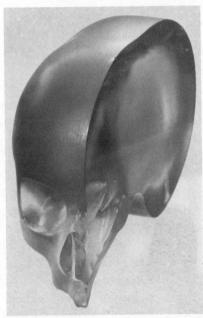

Plastic Skull Sliced in Half for Study
This allowed for study of angles and workmanship,
expecially eye sockets and prism details in roof of mouth.

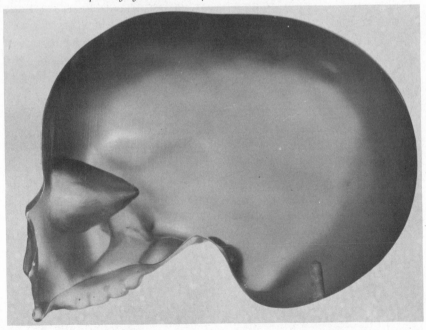

Looking into Polished Cut of Half Skull (Plastic Model)

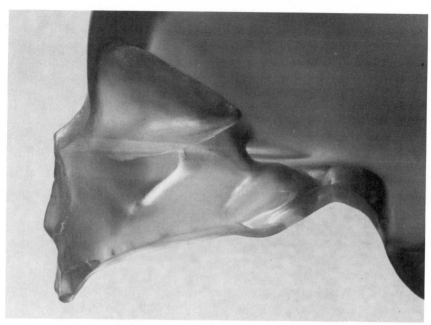

Eye Socket and Prism Close Up (Plastic Model)
The irregular surface contour of eye socket indicates the hand
workmanship—a machine tool would make a smooth outline.

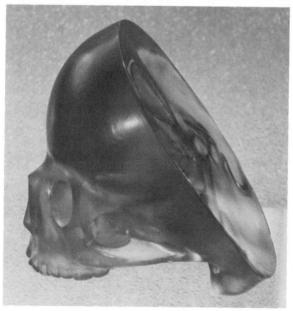

Plastic Skull Sliced at 45° Angle
Made to study eye sockets and inside configuration of skull.

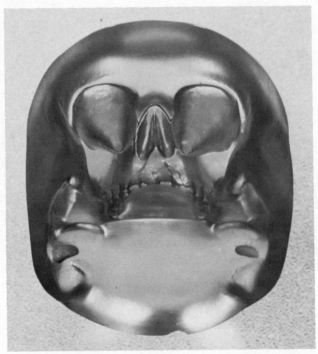

Looking into Polished Face of 45° Specimen (Plastic Model)
Note irregular and "cockeyed" eye sockets and two carefully
drilled holes to support moving skull on two pin axles.

ing effects could be displayed within the skull. It possessed all the
mechanical and optical systems to be a fearsome, moving, speaking
"godhead."

As far as can be determined, the crystal skull is the only existing object from ancient times to support the idea that there were
actually mechanically controlled movable objects that could have
been used as "oracles" or divine mouthpieces.

There are dozens of tales from the past of mysterious mechanized gods, manipulated oracles and temple figures from Egypt
and other ancient lands that talked and moved about in front of
the people, but there are no known examples except this single
skull.[2] The crystal skull is a specimen of a highly sophisticated,
mechanically controlled animated talking godhead—a powerful,
hypnotic, mind-capturing figurehead.

To continue our studies about crystal and its effect on the
mind, experimentation with crystal talismans and crystal psychic

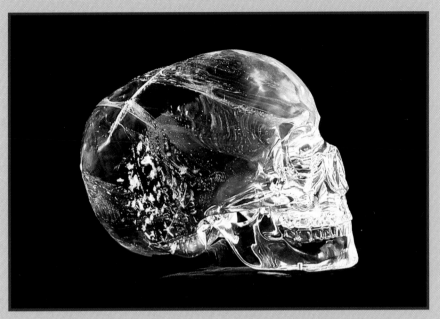

Side View of Famed Mitchell-Hedges Crystal Skull

Three-Quarter Front View of Mitchell-Hedges Crystal Skull

*Frank Dorland Examining Scientific Models
of the Crystal Skull in Marin Studio*

*Sequence of Making a Crystal Ball
Showing raw crystal, the rough cut and finished product*

Recycled Colored Quartz Crystals
These blocks will be cut, carved and polished to form various pendants
and handworking pieces of electronic quartz crystal.

Assorted Electronic Quartz Crystal Talismans
From beginning rough stage to finished product

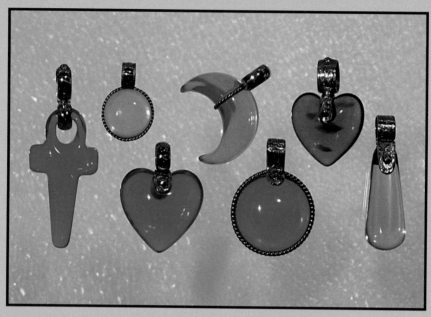

Assorted Electronic Quartz Crystal Pendants

Assorted Crystal Pendants

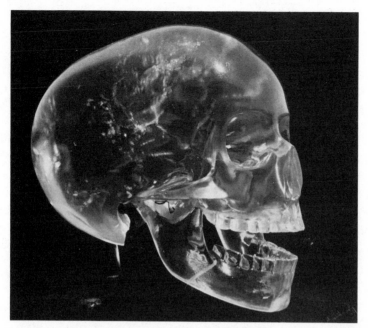

Model of Crystal Skull on Stand Showing Movable, "Talking" Jaw

Hand-Carved Electronic Quartz Palm Pieces

tools became necessary. None of these items were available at that time, so we decided to make our own.

Months of research uncovered very little practical or useful information. We resorted to asking questions in our evening meditations. How were ancient talismans made? What was the procedure? Where did they get the crystals? How many styles were there? Was this common knowledge?

We asked many questions and eventually received satisfactory answers. The answers often came in pictures and occasionally just in a sense of knowing, without words or pictures, just a sensing. By this time, Mabel and I had set up a small experimental lapidary workshop and had successfully cut, carved and finished hundreds of different styles of talismans and working palm pieces. Various seers and psychics cooperated by experimenting with real crystals, and the results were rewarding.

A FEW PROBLEMS

We were in regular communication with Sammy and kept her posted about our activities and progress. She replied with some interesting facts of her own. One issue that we did not discuss with her, however, was our increasing concern about the safety of the skull.

By this time, the skull was receiving generous coverage in the newspapers and on radio and television. It was eventually featured on *Eye on L.A.* (October 1984), *Real People, That's Incredible, Ripley's Believe It or Not* and *Hollywood Reports*, among others.

Its presence in the San Francisco Bay area became known to some of the less savory elements found in every city. We had our share of disturbing telephone calls and several uncomfortable meetings with groups of two to four men who rang the doorbell. They claimed they were students and wished to see the skull for religious and psychic reasons. It was obvious the callers were far removed from spiritual or metaphysical studies. I was grateful that, after each episode, the skull was safely locked up in the Bank of America.

These occurrences made us very uneasy, so we had our three-way alarm system examined and expanded. We also carried additional insurance whenever the skull was displayed or transported.

Our policy stipulated that the services of an armed guard were necessary. This requirement was solved through the cooperation of the Mill Valley Police and the Marin County sheriff's office. We will

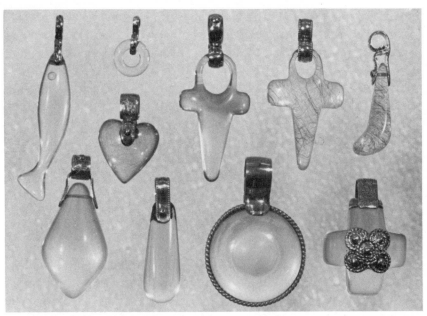

Electronic Quartz Assorted Hand-Carved Talismans

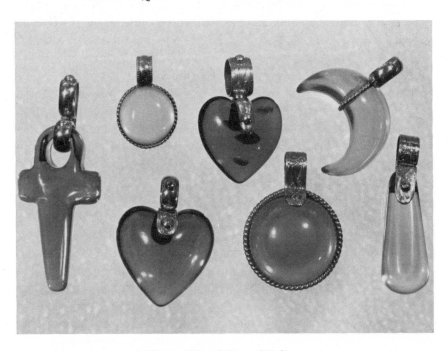

Additional Hand-Carved Talismans

always be thankful for their understanding and help.

We later discovered that at least two plots to steal the skull had been made. A group that met in nearby Sausalito was identified as being associated with fringe Satanic movements. There was also a religious sect with a leader who felt the skull was an evil object and a tool of the devil. He said that the skull should be smashed to pieces before it worked its destruction on San Francisco.

About this same time, the skull and I were guests on a San Francisco television show with a popular female psychic known as the "Dutch Housewife." During the show, she looked deeply into the eyes of the skull and announced in a quavering voice that an earthquake would soon destroy San Francisco and much of the California coast; whatever remained after the quake would be swept away in a gigantic tidal wave.

Although I insisted that the skull was benevolent, and furthermore that it was impossible for it to either cause or control earthquakes, tidal waves, storms or the weather, no one heard me. The listeners had ears for only the doomsday warning of the psychic.

As a result of this unfortunate program, dozens of people sold their homes and left the West Coast for the supposed safety of Arizona, New Mexico and Nevada. It was true that this psychic did receive a warning of death from the skull, but she misinterpreted the entire message. She was quite young, yet she died of a strange disease months later—and not in California. She, too had fled the state in her attempt to escape the destruction she foretold.

We appeared on another television program somewhat later. This time, the station was in Oakland, California, and the major guest star was Pat Boone. The show was pleasant enough, and there were no forecasts of doom. The skull was admired and provided the subject of conversation.

When the program was over, a guard escorted Mabel and me to our car, following us as I carried the skull in its black box. When we left the parking area, a tan station wagon pulled in line right behind us. Soon, we were at the Bay Bridge tollgate heading for San Francisco, and, after paying the toll, I noticed that the tan wagon was still right behind us.

Driving through San Francisco toward the Golden Gate Bridge, I felt sure the tan wagon would turn off at any moment, but the same headlights seemed glued in place right behind us. I didn't feel comfortable anymore.

When our car approached the toll station, I saw a small space in the traffic ahead. I speeded up a bit in the fast lane and then abruptly turned into a space to the right, crossing two lanes and pulling up behind a slow-moving truck. The tailing car was caught by surprise, and I saw the tan station wagon shoot ahead of us on the left. There were several men in the car. As soon as traffic permitted, the tan wagon pulled over just ahead of the truck.

I now felt there could be no doubt that they were really after us.

As soon as we crossed the bridge, we knew they could easily drop behind us again on the wider highway ahead.

At the Marin end of the bridge there was a parking turnout called Vista Point. I knew that Mr. Tan Wagon might pull off there and immediately re-enter traffic right behind us.

If he turned off, I had a very short time to try to ditch him or to speed to the safety of the Sausalito Police Station not far ahead.

"Lady Luck" smiled and the tan wagon pulled off at Vista Point just as a large motor home was starting to leave. The motor home pulled into the freeway entry lane and waited for its chance to enter the stream. Mr. Tan Wagon had no choice but to pull up right behind the motor home and wait.

I didn't hesitate. I floored the accelerator and zipped around the truck.

In a few seconds, I turned right on the Sausalito Road and in a few more seconds turned left on an access road which brought us underneath and to the other side of the freeway heading toward San Francisco again.

When we passed Vista Point, I could see the tan wagon just entering the freeway behind the slow-moving motor home heading north, and we were safely heading south in heavy traffic. We crossed the bridge, turned around, and came back again.

To play it very safe, I drove to the Mill Valley Police Station and sat in their parking lot for at least 15 minutes before driving up Panoramic Highway to our home.

While sitting there I thought, "How strange." It was not like a chase on television or in the movies—no screeching of tires, no wild careening cars. I didn't report this event to the Mill Valley Police, because what could I say? It was dark; I couldn't even get their license number. The men meant business for sure; but who they were, I shall probably never know. Within a month, some of our close friends on the mountainside—a neighbor across Panoramic Highway and two neighbors above us—let us know that two men had called at their homes and identified themselves as C.I.A. investigators. They asked a lot of questions about Frank and Mabel Dorland.

Perhaps some of these incidents were due to an inquiry by some official agency of the government, but I have serious doubts about that. I feel certain that if the C.I.A. or any other government department wanted to know something about us, they would have eventually rung our own doorbell.

We also had a few confrontations at some of our lectures. In one case, the young leader of a gospel church arrived 30 minutes early with his followers. He didn't buy any tickets; he just stood there waiting with his group.

Upon our arrival, the leader approached me cautiously and with a loud, ringing cry shouted, "I here, now and forever denounce you in the name of Jesus Christ." He then looked very startled and anguished, as if he were waiting for me to breathe fire and brimstone at him. I felt so sorry for him that I simply sighed and walked into the auditorium on my way to the lecture platform.

As I lectured, he and his group pulled some outside benches up to the side windows, where they stood on tiptoes to peek in and listen as I talked and demonstrated the uses of electronic quartz crystals. They had disappeared by the time I left the hall.

The effect the crystal skull has on different kinds of people is very strange. I am sure that their subconscious memory banks carried long unused information about this or another crystal skull. This stored data could be awakened by the news or sight of the crystal skull. Some of the cortex centers of the brain could be stimulated, sometimes resulting in strong reactions. Many people were fascinated and almost hypnotized by the skull; some were cautiously afraid of it, but others showed a genuine sense of deep hatred and fear. The skull is not an object to be taken lightly.

As an example, I had some photos of the skull printed by a prominent West Coast printer. When I arrived to pick up the finished work, the head sales manager charged out of his office in an exceedingly agitated state. He began yelling at me, "That's our photo!"

I said no, indeed, that I was the photographer. He then bellowed at the nearest secretary, "That's our picture, isn't it?"

She shook her head, no.

He had beads of perspiration rolling down his forehead as I paid the bill, took my prints and exited as fast as possible.

During our investigations, we had followed standard practices of scientific research and, while they produced no startling discoveries, they generated dozens of clues. In pursuit of these mysterious hints, we also collected and incorporated revealing pieces of information from all *other* available sources.

One major benefit came to us from oral teachings still passed on by many secret societies and communicated to us by some of our visitors. We were told in no uncertain terms that the symbolism of the skull is a death's head to the uninitiated. To the knowledgeable, however, it means great wisdom coupled with full understanding. This helps illuminate the ascending pathway to complete fulfillment.

A RESEARCH CENTER

The biggest obstacle to our research was the lack of available factual material covering religions and their beginnings. Of course, there are some great religious libraries holding countless numbers of fascinating volumes. The bulk, however, is understandably geared to promote and glorify the chosen religion. To the unbiased scholar, it is a Herculean task to dig out true background details. In this respect, a researcher's dream could be a great library covering humanity's beliefs in super beings: the why, when, where and how of origins, practices, laws and effects.

Around 1968, Mabel and I thought it would be worthwhile to form a non-profit corporation as the vehicle to build this badly needed library. We discussed our project with many people and were rewarded with promises of help—both money and fund-raising management.

There was talk of land located on the slopes of Mt. Tamalpais right across the bay from San Francisco. One site had 20 acres near the Panoramic Highway, overlooking the Bay and Golden Gate Bridges, San Francisco, Oakland, Alameda and Berkeley. The price was $1.00 a year for 99 years, revokable if we failed to complete the building and were not in operation within seven years.

Preliminary plans for the building included a circular single-story structure 240 feet in diameter. The crystal skull would be placed at the exact center under a round dome skylight. It would stand by itself on a pedestal surrounded by a 10-foot-wide safety moat. The central floor around the moat would be equipped with comfortable study chairs and large tables sturdy enough to hold many books and papers without crowding.

The outside walls around the circle would be lined with shelves for the available resource materials covering all religions. The necessary offices and facilities would not interfere with the interior, as they would flank both sides of the main entrance.

The intended name of this foundation was the West Coast Metaphysical Center, an institution dedicated to world peace and fulfillment through the power of truth.

This hoped-for research center failed to materialize at that time, but there is no reason it could not yet be done somewhere, with or without the crystal skull.

The role of such a center could be to help refocus humanity's intentions. Modern advancements in scientific warfare threaten all life on this planet Earth. The traditional bending of religious ethics to accommodate political power plays must stop. The future is in delicate balance, and it is increasingly evident that the old orders must fade away and give their strength to the new to insure that there will *be* a tomorrow.

SAMMY RECLAIMS THE SKULL

At the breakfast table one morning, Mabel asked if I knew how long we had been in possession of the skull. I had to reply, "Not really. How long have we had it?" (Mabel kept track of these things much better than I did.) Every so often, I misplaced something and eventually concluded that it was lost forever. Mabel could find it in less than three minutes.

She said that it now had been *six years* since we had brought the skull to California. These six years of research had kept us enormously busy. Together we looked back over our progress, and it was evident that we had discovered as many new mysteries as we had been able to solve.

We continued our research with ever-increasing interest. Then one late afternoon the telephone rang.

When I answered it, a voice announced, "This is Sammy. I'm in San Francisco."

What a surprise! We made an appointment to pick her up at

Anna Mitchell-Hedges with Crystal Skull
Photo by *Mark Chorvinsky,* Strange Magazine

her hotel early the next day. She was ready and waiting for us when we arrived, and we drove her for a short sightseeing tour of San Francisco, which she hadn't seen in many years. Then we drove across the bridge and up the Panoramic Highway to our home and studio far above Mill Valley.

After we talked for a while, Sammy looked at me rather intently and blurted out that I must return the crystal skull to her at this time. She then said, "I am a Catholic. Maybe not a good Catholic, but still a Catholic!"

I was so shocked that I wrote her statement out verbatim and saved it. She then went on to impress me that I could not do any more work with her skull and that she was not interested in anything we had done. She did not want to hear about it, and insinuated that I had been dealing in black magic—using the skull as a powerhouse for personal or evil purposes.

I could not understand in any way how a scientific examination of an archaeological artifact could clash with Catholic teachings. Sammy herself had earlier informed me that the name of the skull was the Skull of Doom and that it could be used to put people to death. On another occasion she implied that she and the skull had done just that to an evil person who was stealing money from poor people.

I wondered if Sammy's imagination had mixed some of her personal thoughts into what we were actually doing. I also realized that Sammy had received letters from at least two sources in the San Francisco area who would have dearly loved to gain control of the skull. I knew they would not have complimented our work but would rather have tried to introduce suspicions into Sammy's mind.

I had reported at length to her about working with several professional hypnotists. We had allowed them to use the skull during hypnotic suggestions with a few selected clients who had serious physical and emotional problems. These experiments were very successful. One hypnotist tried for a long time to lease or purchase the skull from Sammy for use in hypnotic therapy. According to him, Sammy was not cooperative as to either purpose or price.

Since I was an ordained Christian minister, I had Catholic sources who assured me that there was no conflict whatsoever between our research and Catholic conduct. They did want to explain, however, that the common, popular usage and association of the human skull as a symbol of death, spooks and spirits and evil easily influences the majority of minds. I would have to expect that reaction.

Later that day, we drove Sammy back to her San Francisco hotel. Reunited again with her precious crystal skull, she left early the next day for her new home in Canada.

Mabel and I were left with mixed feelings. We had greatly loved our association with the crystal skull; on the other hand, there was a tremendous burden attached to being responsible for someone else's property—especially an irreplaceable archaeological object with a worldwide reputation.

After a few days, we realized that a great weight had been lifted from us. We were now free to concentrate upon our biocrystallographical research. Sammy left us a personal note, thanking us and giving us rights to use any and all information, materials, data, research, photographs and anything else pertaining to the skull with the single restriction that she wished anything we presented to be done in good taste.

A bit later, after Sammy had returned to Canada with the skull, we received a British newspaper clipping from a friend reporting that the Mitchell-Hedges skull had been declared a national treasure of Great Britain.

Mabel looked at me and asked, "How does it feel to take care of a national treasure of England for six years?" We both had a good laugh.

ACADEMIC ATTITUDES

Our original research with the skull had lasted from 1964 until 1970. During that time most of the colleges and universities we contacted showed suspicion and hostility toward us and the skull. We were warned that they did not wish to become involved in any matters pertaining to "anything like that." On two occasions, I was told to keep the skull off campus.

Unique help was in evidence, however, from two professors of the anthropology department of the University of California at Berkeley. The professors were interested and they observed the skull. Furthermore, they furnished us with information which was useful but not generally available.

The trustees and the board of regents at the universities were not so cooperative; in fact, they seemed downright hostile.

Late in 1970, this attitude changed practically overnight. A well-written and researched book, *Psychic Discoveries Behind the Iron Curtain,* became a best seller.[3] The two authors courageously showed how Russia was gaining mental and psychical advantages over the Free World by governmental and university sponsorship of paranormal studies and research into the mind and its control.

It seemed to me that the major American educational institutions instantly reversed their earlier attitudes on the subject. Classes were started under the wings of the psychology departments, and even Stanford University answered letters regarding the Leland Stanford Collection of "apports." (An apport is a physical object which was materialized during a seance in the presence of the medium.)

We even received a most cordial telephone call from a major

West Coast university inquiring into the progress of our research and asking whether we still had the crystal skull available for visitors or showing. We informed them the skull had been returned to Canada many months before.

The investigation had become so complex that it was impossible to complete it as thoroughly as we had hoped by the time Sammy decided to reclaim the skull. The preceding pages have covered some of the highlights of our six years with it. Hundreds of everyday experiences were omitted as insignificant. In like manner, we spent countless hours in many libraries searching for important crystal and metaphysical facts with very limited success. To be sure, many books dealing with the subject were found, but most printed on these issues were fairly useless for our purpose. Crystals and their religious and metaphysical importance were not issues dealt with in any great detail.

We were looking for substantial information and logical, sensible clues capable of unlocking the dual mysteries of the crystal skull and the historical usage of crystals. Eventually, between the oral discussions, research and library studies, we were able to amass thousands of tiny bits of the puzzle. The next portion of this book will deal with certain of the most interesting findings.

EXHIBIT AT ISLE DE NOTRE DAME

On April 17, 1978, I received an unusual phone call from Canada. The caller identified herself as June Regush, author and consultant to the City of Montreal pavilion exhibit. She explained that the 1967 World's Fair grounds on the islands St. Helene and Notre Dame had been in constant use ever since for an annual festival of cultural and educational objectives. It had been so successful that it was recognized and commended by UNESCO in July 1977. It has been called an open window on North America and the world.

Regush went on to say that she was familiar with our work with crystals and the crystal skull. In fact, she had collaborated on a book published just a year earlier that included a chapter on Frank Dorland and the crystal skull: *Mind Search* (New York: Berkeley Publishing).

The City of Montreal, she said, had its own pavilion on the Isle de Notre Dame, and they wanted to exhibit my hand-carved

Electronic Quartz Crystals Sent to Montreal for
"Man and His World" Exhibit

crystals and color photos of the crystal skull. I mailed the photos, and Michael Lambert, design consultant to the city and director of the pavilion, picked up the crystal pieces at Santa Barbara. The exhibit turned out to be a tremendous success—so much so that they ended up purchasing a select group of the crystals for permanent exhibit.

THE FACE ON THE CRYSTAL SKULL

During our many years of crystal research, I personally displayed either the crystal skull or models and photographs of it to thousands of viewers. The common reaction was silence and perhaps awe, but occasionally a rare soul who overflowed with honest enthusiasm would turn to me and say "Wouldn't it be marvelous to be able to see her face?"

I had to agree, for I *had* seen her face several times during meditation. However, revelations of this kind are not usually acceptable as facts. Furthermore, the ability to electronically convert brain-wave activity into graphic portrayal has not yet been accomplished.

One way to put a legitimate face on the crystal skull is through a science known as forensic reconstruction, which has been defined as creating a portrait indicating the original appearance of a former person. The portrait is built on the foundation of the skull or its remnants. This almost new science has made great advances in the last few years and has reached high levels of legal acceptance due to incredible accuracy.

In this connection, I was contacted in 1986 by Frank Joseph, a historical writer in Olympia Fields, Illinois. Joseph suggested showing a model of the skull to Dr. Clyde Snow, who is a renowned physical anthropologist at the University of Oklahoma. Snow's comments would be of great help, so I gladly shipped my plaster cast of the crystal skull to Joseph so he could proceed with Snow on the project.

Joseph reported to me that Snow minutely examined the cast and, after careful deliberations, stated the skull was definitely not simply an artist's conception of a skull, as many have claimed. Quite the contrary, the skull was a carefully made copy of an actual skull of a young female being. This classification by Snow added fuel to Joseph's project, and he was even more intent to find a top forensic scientist who would undertake a reconstruction of the face on the skull.

Months later, I received a telephone call from Joseph, who told me in an excited voice that he had found what may be the top forensic team today. Furthermore, they agreed to make a preliminary study to determine if they could sensibly go ahead with a facial reconstruction.

The team was Peggy C. Caldwell, collaborator with the anthropology department of the Smithsonian Institute, and detective Frank J. Domingo, composite artist with the New York police. Joseph forwarded the plaster cast to them while I sent a set of 8″ x 10″ glossy photographs of the skull to help them in their work.

In due time, we received a report of the preliminary examination, which disclosed that the skull was a copy of a real skull of a young female of the Mongoloid race who was between the ages of 25 and 29 when she met her death. The team could now proceed with the actual reconstruction of the face, which would have been pointless if the skull had turned out to be merely an artist's conception.

The actual facial building process is quite detailed and lengthy. A simple explanation might indicate that known anatomical reference points and the tables of the various depths of soft tissue are carefully followed. The layers of muscle, flesh and skin are laid over the bare skull until the facial features are finally complete.

After a few weeks, we received a final report from Peggy Caldwell and a photo of the drawing made by detective Frank Domingo. The face on the crystal skull is reproduced on the following page. Very likely, the Mayan Indians never saw the young lady, as she probably died thousands of years before the dawning of Mayan civilization. The crystal skull had been handed down to them by an older race who had immortalized their goddess by copying her skull in everlasting quartz crystal, which does not age or decay.

Interestingly, the drawing is basically the face I have seen in meditation, with some differences. The young lady I saw had loose, informal tresses. The color was brown with gold highlights rather than the dark, formal hairdo shown in the official drawing. In addition, her eyes were wide open and expressive.

In my opinion, this contribution by Joseph, Caldwell and Domingo offers valuable clues and insights into humanity's history. The findings on the crystal skull face oppose a widely promoted teaching that, historically, only a great male hero would be important enough to warrant commemorating with a skull carved from solid rock crystal.

When I first saw the forensic drawing of the skull face, I was totally fascinated because of its haunting resemblance to the face I had earlier observed during a series of meditations with the crystal skull. The two faces were different, yet there existed such a strong look-alike feeling I had difficulty dismissing the incident.

After several weeks had passed and the similarity still troubled my mind, I decided to sketch my own "mug shot" version of the face viewed during my own meditations. I reasoned that, if the two drawings were placed side by side, a more logical comparison could be made. We also realized that this would not be any "scientific" proof, but the experiment should be at least interesting. I am not trained in the forensic sciences, so my efforts were limited to

Forensic Reconstruction of Face on Crystal Skull

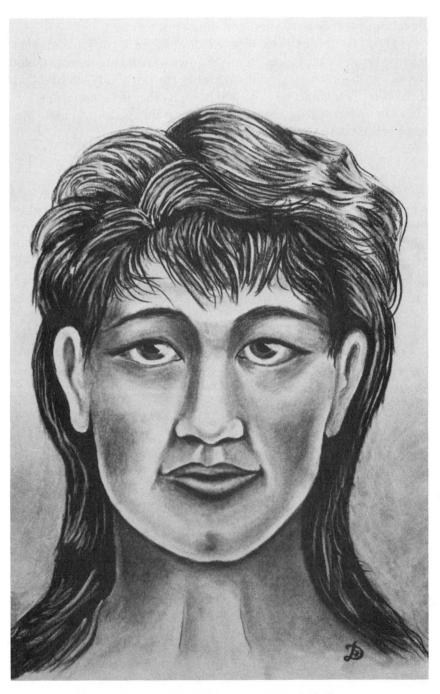

Meditative Vision of Face on Crystal Skull

sketching the face in the stylized mug-shot format.

I hope the forensic scientists will forgive my intrusion and what may be errors of omission. In my attempt to compare mental metaphysics with forensic scientific standards, the possibility evolved that these two fields could be of benefit to each other in certain cases.

The two faces are reproduced here so the reader can make his or her own comparative thoughts.

CRYSTAL SKULL THEORIES

Since 1950, we have explored dozens of old and new theories regarding the skull's origin and history. The silliest one is the belief that the skull was cast from a master mold using liquid quartz made by melting hundreds of small crystals.[4] Rest assured, the Mitchell-Hedges crystal skull was fashioned out of one solid block of left-hand natural crystal. (Crystals naturally grow both left and right-handed.) When crystal is melted, it loses its crystalline structure and becomes a piece of glass.

One theory has been advanced by a prominent university professor, who, although he has never seen the skull except in photographs, insists it was made in Japan in the late 19th century.

Another is that the crystal skull is an anatomical model purchasable from a large German medical supply catalog. This startling revelation came direct to me from a high-ranking museum official after a five-minute visual examination.

Yet a different theory is that the skull was looted from the Holy Land during the Crusades by the Knights Templar, supposedly brought back to London and kept there as a godhead. During the Templars' times of trouble, the skull, along with other treasures, was hidden in a secret cache in London. It has been suggested that F. A. Mitchell-Hedges stumbled across these hidden treasures and later claimed the skull was Mayan.

An additional scenario came from some old timers who knew Mitchell-Hedges. They believe the crystal skull was spirited out of Mexico by high authorities at the time of the Spanish conquest. The skull, gold and other Mexican treasures were secreted on the Bay Islands off the mainland. Mitchell-Hedges supposedly discovered a portion of this treasure-trove during one of his fishing expeditions in the Caribbean Sea, thus acquiring gold as well as the skull.

One last and somewhat more logical theory postulates the

crystal skull was carved over a great period of time: a sort of evo-
lutionary process that took place in several areas of Mexico and
South America and involved at least three different civilizations.
The original raw chunk of crystal from which the skull was created
was found in what is now called Calaveras County in California.
Other large crystals of a like nature comparable with the skull crystal are found there. This is how the story might go:

About 12,000 years ago, a small wandering tribe was foraging
in a riverbed after the spring thaws. They had traveled far for food
and were on the west coast of North America.

A young female member spied a large, melon-shaped boulder
that seemed to speak to her. She came closer to the boulder and
became very excited because the sunlight passed through the solid
rock. She called to the tribe and they came to her side. They also
saw the miracle. They believed that perhaps this was a sign from
God, a grand message from the divine spirit in the sky.

With this important discovery, the young girl became an
instant goddess, and the melon-size crystal, although very heavy,
was carried along wherever the tribe went. The goddess and her
heavenly powers certainly must insure their safety. With time, she
had appointed guardians and escorts who protected her and carried her large, transparent rock that let the sunshine through.

As winter approached, the tribe went south in search of food
and warmth. Eventually, they found a huge cave to convert into
tribal headquarters. A fire at the entrance protected those inside
and gave light through the night. The goddess was delighted to
find she could see the firelight dancing and sparkling in the transparent, divine rock.

As the years rolled by, small transparent rocks much like the
large one were found in dry stream beds and brought as gifts to
the big one. Eventually, a few accidents happened with the small
rocks, and this showed the guards that they could flake off tiny bits
of rock by tapping the pieces against each other. The tapping craft
enabled them to make rough shapes out of shapeless rocks. With
practice and much patience they made ceremonial knives, spear-
heads, arrowheads, fishhooks and other items out of the small,
transparent stones.

After a long time, one of the more gifted artist-guards carefully tapped two rough eyes at just the right spot into the great

crystal. It thus became even more important. It now had eyes to see.

Generation after generation passed while the great crystal remained safe as a heaven-sent protector for its people. Word about the mysterious magical crystal with eyes traveled to other tribes. Soon other spiritual leaders hoped to find a crystal to bring magic to their own people.

In time, the spiritual hierarchy became more sophisticated. They reasoned that God was the creator of all things and that God must reside in the heavens. Since this God was the Creator, God must be female, because the feminine principle creates all life. Obviously, God is She, the Great Mother, the Queen of Heaven.

A Mother cannot be a mother without a Father, so naturally, since the heavens were Mother, the Earth must be Father. Father Earth and Mother Sky; between them they created all things everywhere. In their simplicity the ancient people believed they understood the Cosmos.

In later times, these roles were sometimes reversed. Even today, we hear of Father Sky and (especially) Mother Earth. However, the original scheme can be seen in various early mythologies, such as that of ancient Egypt (e.g., Geb and Nut).

As the spiritual leaders and the guards fine-tuned their skills at crystal working, the Great Crystal was eventually shaped into a beautiful female skull. This was a universal symbol of God, the Great Mother, the Queen of Heaven. They wisely refrained from putting skin on the skull, because they knew the Great Mother was for everyone. If they put skin on her, the people might think that God was of a brown-, yellow-, or red-skinned race. But they knew that God is all of these.

Many researchers believe that the crystal skull originally came from the Isola Mujeres, the Island of Women, which is located just off the eastern tip of the Yucatan peninsula. The Spanish conquerors named this uninhabited island after its numerous free-standing statues, which all portrayed the same woman. At the southern end of the island, they discovered a small stone temple which has since been identified as an ancient shrine to Ixchel. Its dark confines perfectly suited the oracular crystal skull of the moon goddess. (The moon is associated with quartz crystal, usually in the form of clear rock crystal.)

These same associations occur on the other side of the Atlantic.

Egypt's Isis was known as *Regina Coeli,* and the later Roman Juno (Hera of the Greeks) was called the Queen of Heaven. It would seem that, in ancient times, the female figure was held in such high esteem that it took its divine place high in the realms of heaven. Many researchers believe that the mother and child figure so prominent in many religions can be traced back to much earlier times than the Egyptian period. Matrona was an early goddess of the mother and child. In prehistoric times, it seems that the creator of all things was originally deemd to be a great goddess with many mysteries.

Many eons later in a much different civilization, we find male priests predominantly in charge in the temples. The priests were ambitious and wanted more power. They reasoned that, if they dared to cut the solid jaw loose from the skull itself, they could animate the jaw and thus make God talk.

Less than 1,500 years ago, perhaps, this was finally done. The solid crystal jaw was carefully cut loose, beautifully shaped and crafted. The crystal skull was then mounted on two pivoting axes and balanced so it could nod and swing from side to side. The jaw was manipulated by push rods and, due to the balanced skull, the jaw could be moved up and down and the skull's gaze could sweep back and forth as it talked.

This controllable, animated godhead was placed near altar fires to illuminate the sparkling crystal. It was an exciting sight to behold—a beautiful crystal skull with flashing eyes, swinging its gaze over all the people, its jawbone moving up and down in synchronized orchestration to divine orders barked out by the attending priesthood.

This condensed speculation about the crystal skull's origin, evolution and usage is not simply daydreaming. It came about from assembling thousands of pieces of the puzzle into one picture.

I believe that the crystal skull was hand-chipped from a single massive chunk of left-hand quartz crystal that originally weighed more than 20 pounds. The crystal very likely came from Calaveras County, California. The finished piece weighs approximately 11 pounds, 7 ounces. It measures 4-29/32 inches wide by 5-13/16 inches high, and is 7-7/8 inches long. As you can see from the below table, the dimensions of the crystal skull are not greatly different from many actual human skulls.

CRYSTAL SKULL MEASUREMENTS

Glabellar-occipital length	174.0 mm
Maximum calvarial breadth	140.0 mm
Cephalic index	80.5 mm
Bizygomatic breadth	117.0 mm
Nasal breadth	24.0 mm
Left orbit breadth	37.5 mm
Left orbit height	33.5 mm
Left orbital index	89.3 mm

Positive scientific standard measurements are difficult to make, because the skull lacks the normal sutures on the top of the dome. The sutures are missing because the skull was used much like a crystal ball—as a divining crystal. Sutures or any surface scratches would inhibit projecting the mind into the interior of the crystal.

NOTES

1. For more information, see *The Message of the Crystal Skull* by Alice Bryant and Phyllis Galde (St. Paul, MN: Llewellyn Publications, 1989).

2. Of course, there are modern examples such as marionettes, which evolved from ancient religious productions that used animated mechanical performers suspended from strings. These were called "Little Marys."

3. *Psychic Discoveries Behind the Iron Curtain* by Ostrander and Schroeder, Prentice-Hall, May 1970.

4. A temperature of more than 1,723° centigrade is needed to melt quartz crystal.

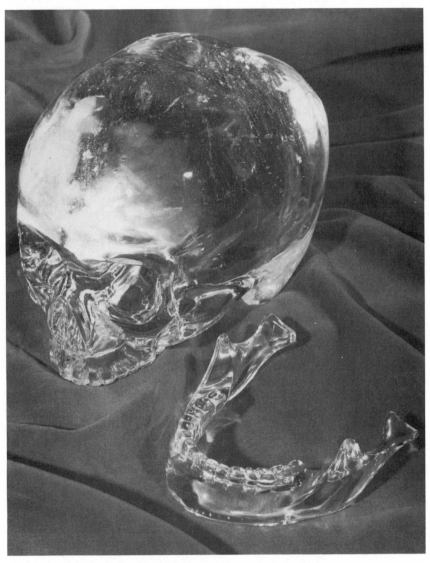

Crystal Skull Showing Detached Jawbone

Crystal History

Fascinating historical tales dealing with crystal are included in this second portion of *Holy Ice.* Like the legends which will be related in the next section, many of these stories have never been written down, or have not been recorded in the form in which they appear here. They are part of an oral tradition related to us by some of the visitors who came to our home during the period when we had the crystal skull in our possession. Although many interesting stories are intentionally omitted because not enough information was available to make a logical report, a few short examples follow.

IOLITE AND VIKING NAVIGATION

I have heard legends that the Vikings were able to make many long voyages to far distant lands because each ship had a working crystal as a reliable navigational device. Fact or fable? How could a quartz crystal be used in navigation?

Conjecture leads us to a possible compass crystal—iolite, also known as cordierite and dichroite. Iolite is found in both Norway and Finland, and has almost identical refractive index and hardness values as quartz crystal. Iolite has a pale blue to dark violet color which may change to pale brown or even brown yellow, depending on the light source. In direct north light iolite displays its deepest blue-violet color, which may change to pale brown or yellow brown with an eastern, western or southern light source.

This color change occurs because ordinary light is made up of electromagnetic pulses that interact with the electromagnetic field of iolite mass. The result is a selective absorption of the color rays similar to polaroid absorption, an action called "pleochroism." This mysterious crystal is but one possibility that could be conceived as a compass crystal originating from Viking lands. Was iolite used in this manner? We don't know for sure.

ANCIENT EYEGLASSES?

Too, there were whisperings that wealthy Minoans lounged comfortably in their box seats safely above the arena floor as they watched Cretan captives perform death-defying acrobatics on the backs of charging bulls. The favored Minoans were supposedly able to see visual closeups of the action by peering through large crystal lenses. Could this be possible?

It was also reported that the upper-class citizens in Babylonia and ancient Egypt wore carefully crafted smoky crystal sunglasses to protect their eyes from the sun's glare. Did that really happen, or are the scientific-historians correct in saying that eyeglasses were unknown until they were invented by Salvino D'Armato in 1285?

MOSES AND HIS HORNS

One more example concerns Moses and the Ten Commandments. Supposedly, when Moses went to the mountain top, he wore a close-fitting hood-like helmet that supported two long slender crystal horns. Is this just another murky fable that has endured the test of time, or could it be possible that Moses the magician possessed some type of antenna used to tune in the Divine? Legend or fact? We do not know. The question is merely raised.

GLASS—IMITATION CRYSTAL

Because of our difficulties in purchasing an authentic quartz crystal ball, Mabel and I wondered about the history of imitating real crystal. We thus began a study of the glass industry. Glass making has been practiced for the last 4,500 years. Museums have existing dated examples from those periods. Glass specimens are found in various colors as well as in clear glass. Blues, greens, yellows, whites, reds, browns and purples, both translucent and transparent, are part of the many varieties classified as being 3,500 years old.

Since that time, glass examples have become increasingly complex and sophisticated in form and shape. Egyptian glass dates back to at least 2300 B.C., and Mesopotamian samples of glass also exist from that same period.

Ancient records show that glass was colored from compounds of copper, iron, antimony, gold, zinc, cobalt and manganese. Colored chunks of glass were widely used in similar ways as gemstones. There are excellent specimens of fine, transparent, fake glass gems from as early as 2300 B.C. This fascinating subject matter makes one wonder how many of the ancient jewels were real and how many were glass. Examinations of ancient crown jewels by gemologists indicate a high percentage of classification errors, if not outright fraud in the designation of glass as gems.

One ancient collection of gemstones recorded in the Bible was on the breastplate of the High Priest (Ex. 28:15-21). This breastplate had 12 stones representing the 12 tribes of Israel and also, perhaps, the 12 months. The dimensions of the breastplate were approximately nine inches across and nine inches high. From the description of the stones, each of which was engraved, they would measure two inches or more in length. To any expert on gems, this means that the "diamond" in the breastplate had to actually be a large chunk of very clear rock crystal. Our studies led us to surmise that in ancient times, almost all large stones described as diamonds were actually rock crystals.

ROCK CRYSTAL AND DIAMONDS

Early examples of sophisticated gem cutting and carving occur on ancient Assyrian and Babylonian cylindrical seals, many of which are skillfully and beautifully fashioned from select chunks of rock crystal. These seals were in rather common use by or before 2800 B.C. They were called cylindrical seals because they were carved in the form of a cylinder, and their patterns rolled out upon a fresh piece of clay. These seals were commonly used for tax records.

A favorite subject portrayed was the Babylonian god, Ea. From this same period, well-shaped gems carved of amethyst, lapis lazuli and turquoise were found. The finest examples, executed with great skill and taste, date from 500 B.C. to 30 A.D. During this golden period, the most popular carving tool was a rotating sapphire point. Sapphire dust and fine sharp quartz sand were both used as cutting abrasives.

During the Hellenistic Period in Greece, which began with the conquests of Alexander the Great and lasted about 300 years, gems of a generous to a very large size were popular. The favored stones were hyacinth, garnet, beryl, topaz, amethyst, rock crystal, carnelian and sardonyx. Numerous well-made glass imitations were also found there in large sizes.

Ample examples indicate that the imitation gem trade flourished at that time. Greek writings from the same period tell us that rock crystal was believed to be ice, frozen at such low temperatures that it would never melt. Rock crystal was closely associated with water and, moreover, was believed to have magical powers. Drinking glasses, pitchers and water jugs carved for royalty from rock crystal were far more than merely expensive, fancy containers. They were special magical items to bless, protect and supply an ever-flowing abundance of fresh, sweet water that was vital to life itself. A crystal chalice was believed to insure fresh water forevermore.

After about 300 A.D., the carving art rapidly deteriorated and failed to be of much importance again until the Renaissance. Until the 14th century, almost all gems were cut and carved into smoothly rounded forms. In the 11th century, a transition to faceting began. A few flat surfaces were ground at the edges of gemstones and, occasionally, one at the top. So, gradually, the top of some of the gems had a flat surface rather than the curved cabachon style.

Gem Cutting

About the year 1640, Cardinal Mazzarini, Prime Minister to Louis XIV of France, gave generous patronage to the arts and particularly to the lapidaries. This financial backing resulted in the famous rose cut for gems being developed. This new style of faceting was called the "Cardinal's cut," but soon became commonly known as the "rose cut." This started the entire modern trend of faceted stones. The "rose cut" remained the trade standard for 150 years until a Venetian by the name of Vincenzio Peruzzin devised the "brilliant cut." This latter cut is still used today; however, by 1988, over 1,220 different good designs for faceting had

Quartz Crystal Babylonian Cylinder Seal (c. 2000 B.C.)
Note mystic cross, associated at that time with Marduk.

been cataloged. The older rose cut had a simple flat table with fully faceted sides, usually numbering 32. The more complex and satisfactory brilliant cut has a bezel of 33 facets, plus a pavilion of 25 facets cut below its girdle.

Natural quartz crystals sometimes have naturally smooth surfaces that look as though they had been meticulously polished. A natural quartz crystal with six shiny, flat sides and six shiny triangles converging to form a needle sharp point appears to the eye to have been skillfully faceted. Could it be that the faceting of gemstones was inspired by observing brilliant sunlight reflections flashing from the mirror-like surfaces of a natural quartz crystal point?

Some gemologists believe that the ancient lapidaries had no knowledge of diamonds as separate stones. Diamonds were undoubtedly found in ancient India; however, the workers didn't differentiate them from any other tiny, colorless transparent stone found at the same time. The ancient Indian gem mines were open pits and yielded many colorless white sapphires, rock crystals, dia-

Single-Terminated Natural Quartz Crystal Point

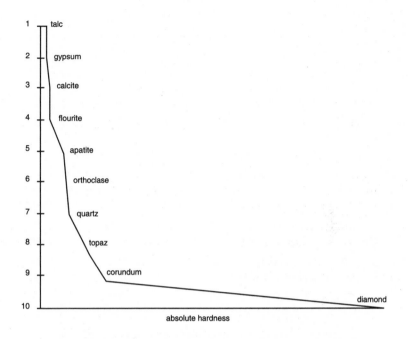

Mohs Scale of Hardness for the Ten Standard Minerals

monds and other colorless stones in the same gem gravel.

The name "diamond" comes from the Greek word *Adamas,* meaning simply "hard and unyielding." Originally, it was commonly used to describe hard metals as well as a mythological invincible gemstone.

When diamonds were found, they were very tiny, difficult to cut, carve and polish, and so were often crushed to produce an abrasive powder for carving. No verifiable records or examples are found of diamonds being used as gems until the start of the 17th century. Very little was known about cutting gems as hard as diamonds before that time. Sapphire was one ancient favorite cutting tool, but sapphire is not capable of even scratching a diamond (see Mohs Scale).

In Brazil, diamonds were first found in the year 1670, whereas the first African diamond was found in 1867. Clearly, diamonds began their great career quite recently. Ninety-nine per cent of the known history of diamonds covers only the last 320 years or so. The remaining one per cent deals with a metal instrument like a pen with a diamond stuck in the end called a *point naive,* meaning "natural." The sharp-pointed diamond was used to scribe on glass, gemstones or precious metals. Whether the point was a diamond or colorless sapphire is debatable.

In 1665, visibly acceptable diamonds were never cut or carved but were left in their natural form except for polishing. If a diamond had visible flaws, Indian lapidaries devised a pattern of grinding flat surfaces on the face of the diamond to cleverly conceal the flaws.

All the noted diamonds have been found in recent times. The famous Culinan Diamond was discovered in the Transvaal in the Union of South Africa in 1905, and weighed a massive 3,186 carats. Other large diamonds were Indian in origin, such as the Orloff, the Hope Diamond, the Great Mogul, and the Shah.

Perhaps much of the reputation of diamond was inherited and intentionally adopted from ancient legends about rock crystal and its mystical powers. Quartz has been used for more than two million years and diamonds for less than 500 years.

THE PHILOSOPHER'S STONE

A Philosopher's Stone turning lead into pure gold—such is the dream loved and pursued by many seekers. Alchemists have vainly followed secret directions compiled from mystical writings and tales in efforts to duplicate this feat. In Europe, they were called "huffers and puffers" because they huffed and puffed in their chemical laboratories as they blew the flames with bellows. They made all sorts of experiments to unravel the mysterious secret of turning lead into pure gold. Were the instructions to be taken literally or symbolically and allegorically?

I believe that turning lead into gold had a spiritual and mystical meaning rather than a literal, material message. The miraculous Philosopher's Stone has already been mentioned in connection with the crystal skull, which may have been an example of such a stone.

The secret is a simple matter, actually. Symbolically, alchemy is to free the shackles of the mind, to transmute a dull leaden individual into a shining, golden light. Transmutation is one of the major secrets of many practitioners in the field of mental therapy. Each individual human being is capable of far more than they could ever imagine.

Crystal Skull—the Philosopher's Stone?

This does not mean that every starry eyed soul could pick up the nearest musical instrument and play with the rapture of angels, but the human mind in most normal, healthy individuals has capabilities far beyond their wildest dreams, and unrealized abilities may be actualized.

THE STONE OF THE WISE?

The crystal skull is a strong candidate to be a Philosopher's Stone because it is a symbol of the human soul in all its magnificence. The crystal skull is a symbol of the mind and its capabilities. Without flesh, no observer could preprogram its classification to a racial group such as Caucasian, Mongoloid or Negroid, rather than a mystical supreme symbol. The skull is merely a parking place for the soul, the mind, the brain, the intellect, where they are housed. The skull is the container.

The stories about the Philosopher's Stone could very well have originated from ancient tales of the crystal skull, a magical stone that turns dull minds into philosophical ones. With age and changing values, the story became distorted and debased into the search for the yellow metal.

In view of this theory that the crystal skull is a symbolic representation of the Philosopher's Stone, it is fascinating to note that the crystal skull was carved from a massive chunk of genuine rock crystal, a gigantic task that took an enormous amount of time. The major reason behind this fascination is that quartz crystal is the only natural material known to man that affects the human mind by broadcasting electronic impulses compatible with and receivable by the body cells and the mind itself.

Perhaps, if it were the original Philosopher's Stone, the crystal skull could symbolize freedom of choice for the human mind and mental potentialities. Masses of people follow their careers by living and acting out what other people have told them they can and cannot do—virtually sleepwalking through life. Every once in a while, we have a rare exception, and then a great leader breaks forth. Sometimes, the exception just didn't realize they shouldn't or couldn't do something and so they went straight ahead beyond limitations to victory.

SEVEN SECRET STONES

During the Middle Ages, church altars were often inlaid with seven sacred stones. These ecclesiastical gems were huge compared to modern sizes; they frequently measured from one and a half to two inches in length.

The first stone was a diamond, symbolizing strength. The second was a blue sapphire, signifying wisdom. The third was a green emerald for adaptability. The fourth stone was a topaz and represented knowledge. Number five was jasper selected to portray beauty. The sixth was a ruby, which depicted devotion, and the seventh was an amethyst to represent prayer and adoration.

Gemologists insist this list is badly flawed because diamonds, rubies, emeralds and sapphires just don't usually come in two-inch sizes. They suggest that substitute stones were commonly used and then incorrectly labeled.

If indeed this were the case, the diamond could have been rock crystal. The blue sapphire may have been either tourmaline, aquamarine or even blue cryptocrystalline quartz. The green emerald was green smoky quartz crystal and the topaz was very likely citrine quartz crystal. The red ruby could have been a massive red garnet or a rare type of red crystal sometimes called strawberry quartz. The jasper and the amethyst would have been genuine jasper and amethyst.

Moreover, it is most intriguing to note that five out of the seven sacred church stones could easily have been active electronic crystals. These five are the clear rock crystal, green smoky, citrine, strawberry and the amethyst quartz crystal. The remaining two, jasper and the blue cryptocrystalline, also belong to the quartz family, although of course they are not active electronic crystals because they lack the proper structure.

Seven is a sacred number of great interest. There are seven musical notes and seven chakra glands that correspond to the seven colors, the seven planets and seven metals. The anima mundi, the universal soul, has been represented as being a sevenfold cross. Its seven parts are consciousness, light, heat, electricity, magnetism, radiation and motion. Number seven is the numerical symbol for life eternal; this meaning can be traced back as far as ancient Egypt. Number seven is called the number of numbers, because a square or a cross is number four, add the Trinity, which is the triangular number three, and the sum is seven.[1] Could crystal, silver and the number seven be linked together for mystical purposes?

EXAMPLES OF CRYSTAL SPHERES FOUND IN THE ARTS

Located in the Prado Museum is a famous painting by Hieronymus Bosch (1450-1516), a triptych known as *The Garden of Earthly Delights,* one of his most inspired works. This painting demonstrates his insistent theme of earthly temptations with a final redemption through the mediation of the Word of the Creator. The inside scenes of this triptych have been illustrated in numerous publications, but a most interesting revelation is found only when the triptych is closed. On the outside of the work a hollow crystal globe is shown that holds the world on the third day of creation. In the center is an island covered with new vegetation. Out of the surrounding waters strange primeval forms emerge near the shoreline.

We wonder if Bosch belonged to some esoteric sect that kept
alive the earlier beliefs of the Great Mother and her hollow crystal
spheres, or if this were a fantastic revelation from his subconscious
mind. The subject of the hollow crystal sphere and its divine association is too meaningful to be dismissed as only another peculiar
coincidence.

NOTES

1. There were also the seven celestial spheres, after which the seven days of the
week are named. Sunday is obvious; that is the sun's day. Monday is moon day.
Mars Day is Tuesday from the Germanic Tiwes (or Tyr's) Day. Mercury Day is
Wednesday from the Germanic Woden's Day. Jupiter's Day is Thursday—Thor's
Day. Friday, Venus Day, is named after the Germanic goddess Frigg or Freya, and
Saturday is Saturn's Day. These are the seven days of the week, the mystical seven
again. There are the seven-headed dragon, the seven altars, the seven loaves, the
seven cities, the seven deadly sins, the seven hills of Rome, the seven seas, and the
seventh heaven. Seven means totality, fullness and completeness. The Revelation
of St. John in the Bible is full of sevens: the seven lamps, the seven churches, the
seven stars, the seven spirits, the seven seals, the seven trumpets, and on and on.
No wonder the number seven is deeply engrained in the subconscious mind.

Crystal Legends

MAGIC AND RELIGION

Magic, mysticism, prophecy, poetry and the supernatural are compatible companions, because they help open a porthole into another world of dreams and visions. Due to its self-imposed restraints, modern scientists are able to sense only a partial slice of the pie of reality. Others are searching for the complete philosophical vision of absolute reality; they are searching for the whole pie.

Classical magic is an art that includes soothsaying and controlling events, forces and effects by employing "supernatural powers." It should be clearly stated that once the "supernatural" is understood, it becomes a natural law. (It is natural to our super nature.) Hocus-pocus nonsense is clearly reserved for the uninitiated. Barnum made a fortune using it.

Depending on times and conditions, a magician could be a major or minor god, a miracle worker, clairvoyant, prophet, seer, wonderworker, priest, wizard, soothsayer, enchanter, medicine man, diviner, shaman, etc. Magic is a basic and integral part of mankind's history.

The word "magic" can easily be traced to the ancient Persian word *magus*, which is the singular of *magi* or magians. A magus is a wise man, a highly educated and intelligent being, a great adept of the occult world.

Megas is ancient Greek meaning "great." *Magos* is a sorcerer and *magikos* is "magical." *Mageia* is Greek, *magice* is Latin and *magique* is ancient French. *Magic* is Middle English terminology. The word magic is now taken to mean the art of an entertainer, a showman who uses sleight of hand and deceptive trickery, which has little to do with its original meaning.

Magic has two opposite practices—black and white. Black magic indicates energies gone wrong or power used for negative and evil purposes. Most sorcery is felt to be this kind of magic. White magic is usage of the highest and purest energies for beneficial purposes. Quartz crystal is a classic mainstay of the highest forms of white magic.

If one were to compile a list of ancient magicians, the topmost one would have to be the original Queen of Heaven, the Great Mother, the Creator (Creatrix) of all things. She ruled as a benevolent and fruitful deity. She was eventually replaced by the Father symbol, an invisible king and protector. The roles switched, for what had been Father Earth became the Father Divinity in Heaven, while the Queen of Heaven was altered to become Mother Earth. Unfortunately, the priesthood gave the divine Heavenly Father the role of a god of jealousy, wrath, judgment and damnation.

Next came biblical figures such as Moses, David and the Savior and miracle worker, Jesus. The Bible has many true magicians who rightfully could be called members of the Great White Brotherhood. A contemporary of Jesus, Apollonius, was another great miracle worker. Others since then were Abraham the Jew, St. Thomas Aquinas and Saint Francis.

More recently, we find Eliphas Levi, who has been called the "last of the Magi." Paracelsus, Agrippa, Michael Meyer, Robert Flood, Philalethes, Cazotte, Lascaris, Ganneau and Louis de Saint Martin are a variety of others who might also claim that title.

Major religions consist primarily of faith, beliefs and appeals to a higher power such as a god, goddess, or a group of gods. Magic, on the other hand, is believed to be based on secret natural laws that operate with precise repetition when the requirements are properly fulfilled. (The concept of modern science is based on these ancient rules of magic; i.e., the experiment is repeatable ending with the same results.)

After a comparative study of the historical uses of magic and religion, one might conclude that the two have common roots interwoven. As far as man's subconscious memory bank is concerned, I believe that magic and religion should be dealt with as a single subject matter.

THE FABULOUS FOUR

Water, crystal, silver and the moon are called the "Fabulous Four." They have been the primary physical elements dealing with religous and metaphysical mysteries.

The Fabulous Four and Religion

The fabulous four elements of water, crystal, silver and the moon were considered necessary for many religious rites. These ceremonies generally took place at night under the sign of the moon. One major reason was because daytime activities were generally endeavors of industry. As long as there was precious sunlight to see and work by, individuals were supposed to be hunting, fishing, plowing and planting, weaving, preparing food, harvesting, or pursuing similarly productive tasks necessary to fulfill their physical needs.

After the sun had set, the magical and spiritual side of man could then be nourished. Nighttime was the preferred time for singing and dancing, drinking and feasting, dallying and lovemaking as well as for prayers, meditations and religious exercises of all types. It should be recognized that singing and dancing have been religious procedures. The hierarchy wisely understood that active congregational participation charged the batteries far greater than sermons.

Water

Rock crystal has always been closely linked with water, because it was originally thought to be frozen holy water that God spilled out of Heaven as a gift to mankind. So, rock crystal was actually "Holy Ice." Water is the first principle of all things, the symbol of the unrevealed God, the divine liquid that nourishes the Tree of Life, and the emblem of eternity encircling all things. Fountains of water are sources of wisdom, because the fountain is the symbol of the soul. A fountain moves/channels living, fresh sweet water, the true elixir of life; the living water that is divine. A flowing fountain of water is an emblem of the Virgin Mary. Fountains are the source of fertility, the waters of life. So fountains are a constant source of youth and rejuvenation.

One of the earliest and most unique examples of a fountain of perpetual youth is that of Kamathos at Argos in ancient Greece. The beautiful goddess Hera was transformed into a virgin again each year as she annually immersed herself in the waters of this legendary fountain.

The sea is the symbol of the depths of the mind; the restless, formless waters constantly swirling in currents, changing from violence to placid calmness in a short period of time. There is an old Irish saying that advocates living by the side of the sea because, "It stops old wounds from hurting, it revives the spirit, it quickens the passions of mind and body, yet lends tranquility to the soul."

Water is the source of all life, and water has always been associated with the female element and creation. Life itself was first born from the primordial waters. In Greek mythology, Aphrodite was born from the froth of the sea. In India, Lakshmi, Vishnu's consort, the zenith of feminine beauty and power, was born as a fully-developed charmer from the churning foam of the sea. Water nymphs, who were beautiful little creatures and the pulse beats of nature, were always associated with sacred rivers.

In the Kabbalah, the Tree of Life depicts the third sphere, the Sefirah Binah, as the Mother, the Great Sea, and also the Understanding and Intelligence of God. Water is used for ritual purification and cleansing, for baptism and renewal, and as a symbolic defense against evil forces.

Flowing water symbolizes the rivers of the mind, the wellsprings of the depths of the subconscious flowing out to nourish the conscious mind. Water is also eternally linked in symbolism with the moon, the constantly flowing tides of the rhythms of life uniting time and motion in eternity. Quartz crystal, in turn, is the mystical mineral symbol of water.

> O thou water, be to us quickening and bring to us fresh power that there be known to us great joy. What fluent blessing is thine? Let us partake of it here like the loving divine goddess mothers. Thee we approach in the name of him to whose dwelling thou dost speeding go. Give us, oh water, of thy strength.
>
> —*Rig Veda*

For the Lord thy God bringeth thee to a good land, a land of brooks of water, of fountains and depths that spring out of valleys and hills.

—Deuteronomy 8:7

And He showed me a pure river of water of life clear as crystal and let him that is of thirst come and whosoever will, let him take the water of life freely.

—Revelations 22

A fountain of gardens, a well of living waters and streams from Lebanon.

—Song of Solomon 4:15

For with thee is the fountain of life; in thy light shall we see light.

—Psalms 36:9

Dragons

Some dragons have always been associated with water so we should, for the moment, review a few stories about these creatures and their mystical meanings. The dragon as a symbol is known in the earliest recorded history. Ancient Babylon displayed carved dragons at its city gates. The dragon is a common sign in ancient Egypt, in India and in China where it is considered the sign of prosperity and good luck.

The word dragon is derived from an ancient Greek word meaning "to see." One reason for this is because dragons can see with their eyes tightly shut, but they always sleep with their eyes wide open. This makes dragons very useful for what seems, in the Western world, to be their most common purpose: that of lurking in deep caves and guarding fabulous treasures.

Dragon scholars trace the roots back to Sumerian mythology which describes a serpent-like being called Zu, which lived in the turbulent, primeval waters ruled over by the sea goddess, Tiamat. She led her army of ferocious dragons into battle against the gods, and Marduk, son of Ea, god of wisdom and magic, defeated Tiamat and clove her in two. One part formed the sea and the other part formed the sky. Thus, Marduk became celebrated at that time as the God of Creation.

In China, where dragons are most popular, they are rated as highly desirable. The Chinese *Book of Rites* lists four benevolent spiritual animals for the kingdom. They are the phoenix, the tortoise, the unicorn and the dragon.

Four Chinese water gods are known as the the Four Dragon Kings. Each Dragon King lives in his own magnificent crystal palace, deep in the sea. Each Dragon King rules over one of the four seas, so together they govern all the waters of the oceans. They command a grand army of crabs and fish that patrol the bottom of the sea.

The four Dragon Kings are responsible for the distribution of the annual rainfall in their part of the world, and they are much loved and respected. Each stream and river has its dragon king and every well has a small shrine, a place for devotionals to these nature divinities.

The four Dragon Kings are ranked so high in the Chinese list of Divine Spirits that they answer only to the very topmost Father in Heaven, who in China is called the August Supreme Emperor of Jade.

In Japan, the Dragon King lives in a deep secret part of the sea attended by all types of sea creatures. The Dragon King controls the storms, the rainfall and every drop of fresh water.

Dragon Sages

The frequent association of dragons with crystal and water hints at hidden meanings. A little investigation reveals that the word "dragon" is sometimes a coded symbol signifying a sorcerer or a very wise man.

In India, a dragon is a master or a yogi, and in Tibet, a dragon is a *narjol*, which is commonly believed to be a mystic saint of great renown.

Buddhist writers have used the word "dragon" to mean *arhat*, someone who has risen to be a great Master on the highest path deserving of divine glories. So we see a dragon can represent a magus, an adept, a naga, or indeed any wise man who has developed extraordinary abilities. This family of three widely used symbols—the dragon, crystal and water—have been used in many legends because they carry with them the message of a smoothly functioning metaphysical bond.

Dragon and Crystal Ball

The Sea Princess

From ancient Germany comes a love story about a handsome knight and a water princess:

Long, long ago there was a brave young knight who dwelt in his castle by the Black Forest. At this same time, there was a beautiful water princess who lived with her father, the Lord of the Baltic Sea, in his grand crystal palace at the bottom of the ocean.

There was a problem in the palace. It seems that sea maidens were born without a soul of their own, but they could earn one if they were able to capture the faithful love of a human man. With this in mind, the Sea Lord sent his young daughter in search of a true and loyal lover and thus gain her own immortal soul.

Early one day, a brave young knight journeyed forth from his castle. He was soon caught in a sudden storm, so when he came to a fisherman's cottage by the riverside, he asked for shelter. The kindly fisherman invited him inside to sit by the fire while the storm continued to rage. It was there in the flickering firelight that he first saw the young girl who smiled up at him. When he spoke to her, she laughed softly and her laughter was like crystal drops of water poured from a silver goblet.

This water princess disguised in human form was fascinated by this strong and handsome young knight so she set out to capture his heart, which she did. Before long the knight swore his faithful love and devotion throughout all of eternity to his newly found sweetheart. Before spring had arrived, the princess had rightfully earned her very own immortal soul.

The two were blissfully happy for over a year, but tragically the knight became enamored with a raven-haired beauty who regularly attended the long evening dinners at the court. One dark evening the knight betrayed his sweetheart, and because she was a water princess with magical powers, she immediately knew what they had done. Weeping and sick at heart, she slipped softly into the depths of the nearby Danube River and made her way out to sea.

She fled to the arms of her father, who welcomed her home to his shimmering crystal palace. He had expected her arrival and had prepared a place for her. After their tearful but joy-filled reunion, he escorted her to her suite of crystal rooms with turrets overlooking a courtyard of rare seaweeds beautifully tended by crabs and shrimp.

Russian Water Gods

In Russia, the water gods are called the *Vodyanoi*. They dwell deep in the lakes and rivers of Russia. In the depths of their watery kingdom, they live in beautiful palaces carved from rock crystal. These wonderful palaces are ornamented with much gold and silver, and they are lighted by a magical stone that furnishes light for every room and hall in the palace. The Vodyanoi control all of the waters of the rivers, lakes, streams, springs and the rainfall in Russia; and they govern all of these activities from deep in their crystal palaces. It is interesting to note that the Russian version of the water gods is one of the rare occurrences where gold is used with crystal.

Crystal

A magical crystal that gives light is a recurring motif in ancient folk tales. Somewhere in the background of most civilizations there is a legend about a magical crystal that illuminates, guides and protects people from evil. In these tales, water and crystal seem to go together like eternal twins.

The theme of crystals as givers of light has also been found in sacred books. One example is found in the book of Ether in the Mormon Bible. The chief character is Jared's brother who was trying to lead his people to the promised land on the other side of a turbulent and angry sea. On God's orders, Jared's brother's people built eight barges with interior space for all of them and "their beasts, animals and fowl."

These specially built barges were designed to be completely sealed against the winds and the crashing seas, which meant there was no light whatsoever in the interior. In a search for illumination, Jared's brother went to the top of Mount Shelem where he "did molten out of a rock sixteen small stones and they were white and clear even as transparent glass." To a geologist, this means he undoubtedly found a quartz seam with a crystal pocket somewhere at the top of the mountain. He built a fire next to the pocket and the heat fractured it, thus freeing the 16 rock crystal points.

The story goes on to tell how the Lord was entreated to reach out and touch each crystal with his finger, thus giving them light. The finger of the Lord touched each stone and they did "shine forth in the darkness."

Two crystals were placed inside each of the eight barges which gave them light.[1] Jared's brother, along with all his people and their livestock and fowl, were then sealed inside and they started their perilous voyage across the dark waters of the forbidding sea. They were blown before the wind for 344 days until finally all eight vessels were safely tossed ashore on their promised land.

The Urim and the Thummim
Another example of light-giving crystals is found in the Holy Bible, which tells of the Urim and the Thummim. These two mysterious objects were concealed beneath the 12-stone breastplate of the high priest and enabled him to receive communications from the divine. Some Biblical scholars believe these objects were a dark, smoky crystal and a clear crystal carried in a leather sack. The crystals symbolized opposites such as yes/no, left/right, guilty/innocent, etc. By holding the two crystals in the palm of the hand and/or

throwing them like dice, one of the crystals would "light up," thus giving the divine orders to the priest.[2]

In ancient times, colorless stones such as diamonds, rock crystal, white sapphires, or any gemstone that was clear as well as transparent was thought to be one and the same thing—simply a crystal. Any of these might be thought to be the never-failing light that illuminated the temple of the soul.

Healing

For health purposes, both colored and colorless stones were thought to be useful. A precious stone could be ground into powder and taken as a medicine for practically all ailments. Other precious stones might be laid over a troublesome spot such as sore throat or a bad liver and certain magical qualities would emanate from the stone, curing the illness. To prevent disease, the stone could be worn on various parts of the body.

For severe illnesses, especially those affecting famous people, stones were pulverized and swallowed.

When Pope Clement VII was stricken with his fatal illness in 1534, his physicians gave him daily doses of ground, precious stones. In 14 days, the Pope swallowed approximately $100,000 worth of powdered diamonds, rubies, emeralds and other selected stones which undoubtedly helped in hastening his demise.

Modern studies indicate that many illnesses can be overcome by practicing mind control. The body attempts to heal itself if given the opportunity. We do know of one gemstone that does react to mental and physical energies, and that stone is the electronic quartz crystal. My research and experiments have failed to discover any other stone or any other crystal that effectively shows any useful reaction. Many people think that various stones have properties that are good for varying illnesses, but this is applied psychology, not science. Electronic crystal reacts; others don't.

Silver

Scientifically, silver has the highest degree of both thermal and electrical conductivity known. In addition, silver is ductile and very malleable. Silver is a noble metal of great value with possible benefits occurring because of spiritual association with divine power. Silver has been used in lavish amounts in churches and shrines—not ounces or pounds, but many tons of the precious metal in a single building. Most was used for altars, altarpieces, ceremonial objects and all sorts of accouterments.

In some cases, builders started using the sacred silver from the ground up. In ancient Ceylon (now Sri Lanka), the walled city of Anuradhapura served as the capital city for the Ceylonese royalty who ruled from 400 B.C. through most of the 10th century. In the 2nd century B.C., a shrine named Ruvanvali (Ruwanweli) was built there in honor of the Lord Buddha. This pagoda-like structure was the third largest of its kind in all of Ceylon. Remarkably, this shrine was erected on a single 500-square-foot slab, seven inches thick, made of solid pure silver.

In Seville, Spain, there is a 69-foot-high altar crowned with a solid silver altarpiece weighing a ton and a half. This noted religious piece was reportedly used in the 17th century for the canonization of King Ferdinand III. In more recent times, in November 1982, this altarpiece was used by Pope John Paul II for the beatification of Sister Angela de la Cruz who founded a religious order to serve the poor.

Metaphysicians believe that Revelation 2:17 refers to metallic silver. It reads: ". . . and will give him a white stone, and in the stone a new name written, which no man knoweth saving he that receiveth it."

Silver is also the mandatory metal for any buttons, buckles or metallic articles worn or used by wizards, wonderworkers and the like. In addition, it is believed that a werewolf, an evil ghost, a black sorcerer or any spirit of darkness can be killed only with a silver bullet.

An ancient kabbalist manual reveals that heaven is divided into 196 provinces ruled by seven supreme angels. The seventh angel was known as the Lord of the Waters and the Supreme Lord of the Powers of the Moon. With his magical abilities, he had a habit of transmuting anything within reach into precious silver, a symbol of the moon.

Gold and silver are the two leading "noble" metals. Considered opposites, gold is the sign of the sun and daylight, while silver is the mystical, night moon sign. Silver and crystal are both moon signs, so they are compatible in every way.

Silver has a history of being a most favored precious metal for all ceremonial articles of the church and state. For serious metaphysical use, silver is mandatory as well as traditional for all metal implements. Quartz crystal is a vital part of this picture; it is the secret catalyst.

The Moon

The ancients believed that the moon was a powerful goddess passing nightly across the sky exerting a mighty influence on all the waters of the earth. The ebb and flow of tides are precisely governed as she constantly changes her shape, thus visibly marking heavenly changes of time as well. The tides are highest twice a month, at the new and at the full moon.

Since the physical bodies of all living things contain water, the moon was felt to influence life whether recognized or not. The mating instincts of humans, animals, fish and fowl are stimulated in rhythm with the moon's cycles. The spawning of species of crabs, mussels, oysters, worms and grunion can be forecast by moon signs. Observant fishermen, farmers and others whose work brings them in close contact with nature's rhythm pay close attention to these revealing signals.

Metaphysical teachings disclose that the moon is a very significant regulator of nature's timetable. Ancient monuments such as Stonehenge and other circular delineations were agricultural guideposts as well as ceremonial sites. Lunar reckonings mark many events on the calendar, some of which are still followed faithfully. Easter and the Wesak Festival are two examples.

The ancient Chinese believed that the moon was the power behind the Yin "female energies" controlling female reproductive cycles of 28 days. The word "menstrual" literally means monthly (the lunar month, not the calendar month). This cycle is closely linked with the mystical number seven, because the seven days of the week are derived from the lunar cycle of 28 days. When seven is multiplied by the sacred number four, which is the mystical number of the cross, this gives 28. A normal gestation period is exactly nine lunar months. A lunar month is 29.53 days.

The word "lunatic" is derived from the Latin word *luna*, the moon. Countless examples of disturbed behavior during the full moon have been given by firemen, policemen, doctors, psychiatrists and others who work with the public. For centuries, such aberrant behavior has been called "moon madness."

Sociologists have recently accumulated vast amounts of data from reliable sources and fed this information into their computers. The official results disclose that in humans, both males and females go through a regular monthly cycle. The birth rate zooms during the full moon and sexual activity peaks at the same time. On the dark side, crimes such as murder, rape, robbery, car thefts and senseless prowlings and vandalism also increase drastically.

Obviously, the moon has a profound effect upon all living things as well as the human mind (emotions). For better or for worse, the moon goddess gives occult powers and exalts all phases of nature's fertility. She reigns supreme as the queen of the night and the illuminating goddess of the heavens.

The awesome power of the moon over physical matter is evident during the daily tidal movements when untold billions of tons of water change position on the earth's surface. Metaphysicians have long told stories that not only is the water moved, but the earth itself is pulled out of shape from one side to the other as it rotates.

If this is true, then the moon's pull could possibly trigger earthquakes. Records of California temblors show major quakes occurring in 1933, 1952, 1971 and 1987. At each disturbance the moon just happened to be at its maximum lunar declination. In astronomers' language, this means that the moon was at its northernmost point where it exerts the strongest possible force of gravity on the earth.

Salt and Fire

Besides water, crystal, silver and the moon, two more elements are often present at ceremonial events. The additional two were salt and fire. Salt is considered a sacred bond between the spiritual and the physical world. Salt is incorruptible and so is a necessary part of exorcism as well as a vital ingredient in holy water. In ancient times, a small dish of salt was present during devotionals, and this custom is sometimes still followed today. A small dish of salt, a clear bowl of water and a burning candle are three tools of the spirit. The salt should be pure, natural sea salt, not prepared table salt as is usually found at the supermarket, because this product contains special adulterants useful only for manufacturing, handling and storage.

Fire is a prime ingredient of magic and religious ceremonies. The temple fires give light and warmth, and they are the symbols of purification, renewal and resurrection. Fire represents the duality of life and nature—the friend and the foe, the comforter and the destroyer. Fire symbolizes domestic hearth fires and peace and industry, as well as total conflagration.

Sacred fires, divine fires, perpetual fires of the gods and goddesses fill the pages of religious history books. As man emerges out of his dim past, the temple fires and the fires of sacrifice, burning huge mounds of fat from freshly killed animals, slowly dwindled down to the flames of church candles.

In many places, by law, the church candles must contain at least 51 per cent beeswax. This is still true today, even though the votive candles commonly sold are only paraffin. The necessary beeswax content was inherited from the ancient rites of burning sacrificial animal fats. Perhaps the vibrations emanating from the burning fatty parts of animal origin act as an attractive beacon to entities in the spirit world.

If someone wished to gain the attention of friendly spirits, a departed ancestor, loved one or the guardian angels, a beeswax candle would be lit as prayers and incantations were said. Since the world of industry and commerce traditionally extends and adulterates their goods, laws were passed to insure that the church candles contained at least 51 per cent pure virgin beeswax. The remaining 49 percent could be cheaper tallows and paraffins.

ASTERIA, THE STARRY ONE, QUEEN OF HEAVEN AND PATRON SAINT OF CRYSTAL WORKERS

In ancient races, a supreme female deity was worshiped. Certain myths tell about a goddess named Asteria. She was known as the "starry one," the "Queen of Heaven" and the "shining light." Her vibration as the feminine principle exists through time.

The Assyrians had Ishtar, the Arabians had Ilat, the Phoenicians had Astarte, the Greeks later had Astraea (or Asterië), the Star Maiden, as well as Venus and Aphrodite and many others.

Asteria served as a benevolent goddess of crystal workers as well as the Queen of Heaven, Her modern namesakes are the aster flower and the asterisk symbol, as well as the crescent moon and the stars. She was Leto's sister, the daughter of Koios and Phoibe. This pair were the children which resulted from the mating of the earth with the heavens. They were Titans, which means nature powers. Asteria later mated with Perses, and they had a daughter, a goddess named Hecate, who eventually became the patron saint of witches.

Asteria was a mistress of magic and a wonderworker. Her main interest was working with crystal energies, because all the stars in her glittering heavens were considered crystals. Her colors are green and silver with the blue of the heavens. The moon is the earth's satellite and green is the color which represents the earth. Green is also the color representing the moon and this comes from the blue symbolizing Venus mixed with the yellow associated with Mercury.

Green is the classic color for magicians, wonderworkers, doctors, priests, medicine men, shamans and the like. Green, silver and crystal and of course, water, are intimately associated with the moon.

The story goes that at one time the earth was perfectly flat. One could climb any of the high mountains and look down into the valley below to see the earth's flatness. The earth was very precious; to protect it, Asteria magically fashioned a huge, hollow, crystal dome to cover it. She cut holes in the crystal dome to allow the clouds, the winds and the rains to pass through.

To finish her creation she hung millions of crystals by silver threads inside the heavenly dome and called them her stars. The Great She then created hollow crystal globes in which to carry safely the moon and the planets. She placed each one inside its own crystal sphere for safekeeping and suspended them by silver threads up among all her stars.

Later, she discovered that, when the winds blew across the hollow crystal globes carrying the planets and the moon, she would hear celestial harmonies like a great pipe organ in the sky. Asteria called this the "music of the spheres," and the tones delighted her, for this was her own heavenly orchestration.

With time, the silver threads became black with oxidation and could no longer be seen. Today, the stars and the moon and the planets seem to be magically suspended in dark space above the world as Asteria manipulates their nightly travels across her heavenly domain.

DIAMONDS IN THE SKY

Ancient people believed that the twinkling stars were crystals suspended on silver threads hung from the top of the heavens. In 1992 at the annual Lunar and Planetary Science Conference held in Houston, Texas, NASA scientists made an astounding report.

An analysis of studies carried out at the Infrared Telescope Facility at the top of Mauna Kea in Hawaii indicated that molecular clouds contain a most unusual carbon atom bonded to a hydrogen atom and three other carbon atoms. Further analysis showed that these immense blobs of gas and dust, which eventually give birth to stars, are full of floating micro-diamonds. The researchers believe that as much as 10 per cent of the carbon present in the molecular clouds is in the form of tiny diamonds.

It is not clear, say the scientists, whether the diamonds came into existence from the explosion of a long-gone star or whether they formed in space in some manner. It is known, however, that diamonds have been found in meteor fragments that hit the earth. It is also fairly common knowledge that heat and pressure under the right conditions can form diamond crystals just as they can form quartz crystals. It is logical to assume that the diamond-lined clouds in the cosmos came from exploding stars.

We also wonder if another study might reveal that the cosmos is also full of tiny, floating electronic quartz crystals—or maybe some big ones. Is it just an accident that ancient people thought the twinkling stars in the heavens were crystals, or did they have some information from somewhere that was lost as time went by?

LEGEND OF THE WHITE LADY

There seem to be many legends in the South American countries that tell of a mysterious white lady who comes out of the sky to live with and help the native people. Here is one of several versions.

Legend of the White Bird

Shortly after dawn on a clear, cold day, a dazzling white bird was seen circling over a flat part of the valley floor near the river. The bird soon swooped down gracefully and landed on the barren soil. In only a few moments the bird had vanished, and in its place there stood a strikingly beautiful lady with milk-white skin. Her spotless, soft, white gown seemed to rustle like leaves in the slightest breeze. When the lady walked, she seemed to effortlessly glide across the ground without quite touching it.

The people in the valley soon came to see the new white-skinned lady, and as soon as they saw her they took her into their hearts with love and awe. As time went on the white lady showed the people how to do many things; to plant and grow food, to sew clothing, to build warm homes, and how to take care of babies and folks when they grew old.

After several years she had them build her a fine palace with enough rooms for the lady and all who wished to serve her. In the center of the palace she had chosen workers build for her a temple with a small, stone altar exactly in the center. When it was finished and the workers had gone, she placed a magic stone on top of the altar. This stone was almost round, and it was as smooth and clear as fresh spring water sparkling in the sunlight. With this mysterious, magical stone, she reigned over her subjects, unconquerable in her serene peace and harmony.

As the years passed, the white lady gave virgin births to three handsome sons who were raised to manhood in the palace. One day she called her three sons to see her in the temple because she had a gift for them. When they were in the temple, she told them she could not stay on earth much longer because she was getting old. She then divided all of her lands into three equal parts and gave each son his equal share. The sons dutifully took over their portions, which they ruled with justice and fairness according to their mother's instructions.

One day the beautiful white lady went into her temple and picked up her magic, water-clear stone from the altar. In a few moments the lady vanished and in her place there stood a beautiful white bird on the temple floor. The bird flew through the rooms of the palace and finally out the window. It flew upwards and slowly circled the palace three times. It dipped its wings once, then ascended higher and higher until it disappeared never to be seen again.

GODDESSES

According to some authorities, one single Madonna or Great Mother was worshipped in the Paleolithic Age. In Sanskrit, there is a word—*lalitásahasranámam*—which means "the thousand names of the Goddess." Also in Sanskrit, the lone word *Srimata* means

"Glorious Mother, Queen of the Universe."

A random sprinkling of later names of the Goddess from different times in different cultures would include Athena, Aphrodite, Freya, Inanna, Ishtar, Isis, Maia, Minerva, Nut, Shakti, Troma, and so on and on. There are many, many more. Truly, She is the "Goddess of a thousand, thousand names."

INDRA'S NET

There is an endless net of threads
Throughout the universe.
The horizontal threads are in space,
The vertical threads are in time.
At every crossing of the threads,
There is an individual,
And every individual
Is a crystal bead.
The great light of absolute being
Illuminates and penetrates
Every crystal bead, and also,
Every crystal bead reflects
Not only the light
From every other crystal in the net,
But also every reflection
Of every reflection
Throughout the universe.
     —From the *Vedas* (the Hindu sacred canons)

There are four books in the Vedas. They incorporate the hymns (Samhitas) the manuals and rituals of prayer (Brahmanas) and the Upanishads, which were the philosophical treatises. The four Vedas are:

1. The Rig Veda
2. The Yagur Veda
3. The Sama Veda
4. The Atharva Veda

Indra of "Indra's Net" is mentioned in the Rig Veda as the King of the Gods and master of the storms, rain, thunder, and lightning.

The Brahmans state that the Vedas were formally assembled and compiled at Lake Mansarovara in Tibet about 1500 B.C. from very ancient teachings handed down through the ages by oral recitation.

Indra was the most prominent of gods in the Rig Veda, the Hindu sacred book of scriptures ascribed by conservative scholars to the second millennium B.C. The Rig Veda is commonly called the oldest of all written literature originally composed from ancient oral recitations.

Indra was lord of the air space between the high heavens and the earth. He was a water and weather god who controlled the storms. The Hindu version of the Great Flood tells of Indra's growing jealousy of the popularity of Krishna. In anger he poured down rain in an attempt to drown mankind.

Indra was also a warrior's god. His weapons were the thunderbolt and the rainbow, which he used as a mighty bow to shoot his terrible arrows of lightning. His skin was of a golden hue. He was carried across his skies in a golden chariot drawn by warhorses who were covered with hair that resembled the feathers of a peacock. This was because at one time he was in danger of being attacked by a violent demon. To escape he turned himself into a peacock and flew away. In a gesture of thankfulness, he gave the bird a thousand eyes in its feathers, the ability to forecast rain and the powers to destroy snakes.

Indra was a heroic god of gods in the earliest days. He was popularly known as the bull of the world and made women fruitful. It was told that Indra had a thousand testicles. At the height of his power he had Vishnu as his faithful and constant companion. Later as his powers faded Vishnu's grew until he finally emerged as the absolute supreme deity. In the sixth century B.C., early Buddhism recognized Indra as the Great Protector. At the same time Brahma was acknowledged to be the great inspiration for the doctrine of Buddha.

THE MAHARAJAH AND HIS TELL-ALL CRYSTAL

A long time ago when India was very young, a Maharajah ruled over his large kingdom in the north. He was a kindly and noble monarch who did his best to help his people. He was also a despondent king, because his subjects were very poor and often hungry; there was not sufficient food to eat. In addition, the

Maharajah had no male heir to leave his kingdom to. These troubles made him brood alone with his unhappy state.

One winter day his Maharani came to him asking to see the royal doctor because she was feeling poorly. The astrological signs were consulted and at the auspicious moment the royal physician was escorted to her bedchamber where she lay waiting to be helped. After seeing the Maharani, the good doctor consulted his oracles and three days later told the king his Maharani was with child.

When this news was spread throughout the palace there was great rejoicing, and royal plans were made for the promised birthing. Whether the child would be the hoped-for boy or another girl was the preoccupation of all the oracles and soothsayers. The king laughed and said he knew, he knew. It had to be a son as he had a dream of a new Maharajah riding into the kingdom on the back of a royal elephant.

The months slipped by rapidly as the Maharani became bigger and bigger with child. By this time summer had arrived and the kingdom was sweltering with the oppressive heat. The Maharani cried out in anguish, then prayed to the storm gods to bring the rains to wash away the heat. The wind arose as the skies darkened. Thunder rolled out of the mountains nearby while the skies loosened torrents of rain. Lightning flashed down repeatedly as wind and rain lashed the earth. An enormous lightning bolt struck a giant tree on the hillside just beyond the castle. This split the tree in two, and the violent winds uprooted the remains.

The babe was born in the palace at the same time the lightning bolt had demolished the tree. Early the next day the storm had subsided. The morning light revealed the split tree lying on the hillside with its roots in the air washed clean of dirt by the driving rains. In the hole where the tree had been there was a giant, clear quartz crystal shining in the morning sun. The tree had grown for centuries over this hidden crystal in the ground.

When this news reached the Maharajah he proclaimed it as an omen from the gods for his first-born son, and the kingdom rejoiced because the baby was a male child, a prince. Fifteen years later, the royal prince was given a birthday party in the palace. By this time he had been trained by royal tutors to eventually take over the kingdom for his father.

In the spring of the year, the Maharajah was taken ill by the spring fevers which annually passed through his kingdom. The fever seemed to be very bad that year because so many of the young, the weak and the elderly had been unable to survive the sickness. The Maharajah's condition worsened in spite of all the various medications given him by the royal physician. In the early hours of the morning of the dark of the moon, the Maharajah succumbed. The kingdom was placed in a period of mourning by the 15-year-old prince, the new Maharajah.

The young king was most apprehensive about his duties until an old crone approached him and whispered in his ear: "Have them bring you your crystal which was uncovered at the time of your birth. It is your birthright. It is a magic tell-all crystal."

"How will I know what to do with this crystal?" asked the young king.

"Ask the crystal; look at it and ask. It will tell you itself," she murmured softly as she turned and walked out of the room.

The newly crowned monarch ordered that the big crystal be carefully dug out of the ground and brought to the palace.

The crystal was so large and heavy that the workers had to make a sturdy, special carriage to haul it to the palace where they put it in the courtyard to clean. The men washed the crystal, and then washed it again and again until it was sparkling clean. They next washed the dirt from the courtyard floor and everyone was amazed, because the paved brick floor was literally covered with shining yellow nuggets of pure gold.

"It is gold!" the men shouted.

"It is gold!" all the soldiers shouted.

The Maharajah came running to see what the commotion was about.

"Gold!" shouted the Maharajah.

Everyone then went out to where they had dug the crystal out, which was now a big hole. A young man jumped down in the hole and scooped up a pail of the dirt. All the dirt in the pail was washed away with water, leaving the bottom of the pail covered with tiny gold nuggets.

Before long there were hundreds of people working every day to dig out the dirt and wash it away, leaving behind the golden nuggets. The kingdom was overjoyed, because they were no longer poor. Everyone would have enough food and clothing, and each family could have their own home.

In thankfulness the people fashioned a six-foot-high throne of solid gold for their wonderful Maharajah. The gold throne sat with its back to the north wall of the royal palace throne room. Directly in front of the throne stood the big crystal, which was just over seven feet high.

The kingdom soon became very rich, the richest in all of India, as each bucket of dirt produced hundreds of small gold nuggets. The Maharajah spent more and more of his time sitting on his solid gold throne looking at his magic crystal. He said he had no need to go anywhere because he had a tell-all crystal that showed him everything that was going on in his kingdom.

One day the Maharajah paled as he looked at his crystal. He called his royal guards and told them they must be very alert, because he had seen a band of thieves plotting to steal his royal throne. The guards promised extra cautious vigilance. They then retired to the guards' quarters, where they laughed at the fears of the Maharajah.

"Who could possibly bother to steal the throne?" they said. "It would take ten mules to carry it."

"If someone wants our gold, there is plenty out at the mine for the taking. All they have to do is wash the dirt."

A few months later a band of men said they had brought 12 baskets of gifts to the Maharajah and they would like to give him his presents. The palace guards let them in to see the Maharajah personally. They then went back to their amusements in the guards' quarters.

The spokesman for the band brought out three small wicker cages containing six doves.

"They are doves of peace," said he.

The Maharajah smiled as he took the three cages to the palace window, where he let the doves loose to fly away.

"Peace goes with freedom," said the monarch happily, as he turned his back to the men so he could watch the doves fly.

Seeing their chance, the nearest man thrust a long dagger into the monarch's turned back. They then fell on him with knives and clubs. In a moment the Maharajah was no more. The men pushed his bleeding body to the corner and piled pillows and draperies over it to hide it from sight. They then took sharp saws out of the gift baskets and cut the golden throne into many small pieces which they placed in the 12 baskets.

"Let us go quietly as fast as possible," said one.

"How about the crystal?" said another. "I hear it is magic. It would tell on us, so we must destroy it."

"It is too large and heavy to move, but if we could smash it into smaller pieces we could throw them out the window into the lake. Then we go free," he cried excitedly.

The men then took several heavy pieces of the sawed-up throne and used them like a sledgehammer to batter the crystal to pieces. This made such a sharp racket the guards finally came running to see what was happening.

A fierce and bloody battle started immediately. They fought on and on until every thief lay dead. Many of the guards were sorely wounded and several bled to death on the palace floor because no help could be given while the fighting continued. The kingdom was plunged into deep sorrow at this unthought-of tragedy.

"How could this happen?" they asked one another. "If they wanted gold, we have plenty to give them. We have more than we need."

By the end of the day the Maharajah's body had been washed and clothed in his finest garments. His body was placed on view in the great room so his subjects could come and say a prayer for him.

In the darkness of the evening, a very old grandmother who had been a lady-in-waiting for the former Maharini stood by the monarch's body with tears in her eyes and slowly said, "There are always some who prefer to work harder to steal, hate and kill rather than help, share and love."

The old grandmother then took a deep breath as she wiped her eyes, turned and walked slowly off into the darkness.

GIANT ROCK CRYSTALS

Giant crystals like those in the foregoing legend are not simply a fictional invention. A large rock crystal was reported in Italy in 1797. Described as being at least three feet in diameter, it was found in the Italian Alps.

The natural history museum in Paris at one time displayed a rock crystal that measured three feet in every direction. It had been found in Switzerland. A clear rock crystal measuring more than

three feet across and more than six feet high was reported in India
in the 17th century. A clear rock crystal found in Calaveras County,
California, around 1860 was reported as being more than three feet
across and more than four feet in length.

Many crystals as long as two feet were reported as being in
the way during the railroad-building days in California. The crystals were blasted out of the ground. The Chinese laborers reportedly gathered up the large chunks and sent them to Chinatown in
San Francisco to be made into crystal balls or sent back to China.

HUNZA, KASHMIR, THE CRYSTAL MOUNTAIN AND SHANGRI LA

Mysteries, myths and legends flourish nowhere else in the
world as they do in a relatively small 1000-mile-long stretch of
land. This magical area starts in the Hunza Valley at the northern
rim of Pakistan and goes eastward to the base of Mt. Everest in
Tibet and Nepal.

Hunza

The Hunza Valley is where the world's four highest mountain
ranges meet. They are the Hindu Kush, the Karakoram, the
Himalayas, the Pamir mountains of China and Tadzhikistan. Their
peaks surround the lush valley which has been almost completely
isolated until recently when a new marvelously engineered all-
weather highway was successfully completed. The new highway
replaces the famed but tortuous Old China Silk Road.

Some believe the Hunza Valley to be Shambhala, the legendary
valley that inspired the modern tale of Shangri La. Other scholars opt
for a lesser known valley, one that is much closer to Mount Everest.

Kashmir

The land of Kashmir has nourished mystery schools for more
than 2,000 years. It lies in the Himalayas between Pakistan and
China, northwest of Nepal. While this territory abounds in rugged
high-mountain terrain, it also has a marvelous fertile valley which
is about 80 miles long and 25 miles wide. This valley is responsible
for Kashmir being hailed as the garden paradise of India. Legends
tell about the Master Jesus being initiated into the mysteries taught
there, because the Kashmir Valley is believed to have been the res-
idence of Jesus for the period of his life not recorded in our mod-

ern Bibles.

Apollonius of Tyana

A contemporary of Jesus was the controversial Apollonius of Tyana (in Cappadocia in what is now eastern Turkey), who was also a student at the Kashmir mystery schools. Apollonius eventually fell afoul of the authorities when he became famous as a magician and wonderworker. He was tried and convicted before Emperor Domitian (Titus Flavius Domitianus, Emperor of Rome 81-96 A.D.). When sentence was passed, Apollonius secretly placed a crystal under his tongue and miraculously vanished before the startled eyes of the court and the guards. He eventually formed his own mystery school, lived out a full, long life and died peacefully at the age of 100 as he had predicted.

The Crystal Mountain

A little over 500 miles southeast of Kashmir lies the sacred Crystal Mountain of Nepal, called Shey. Mysterious, holy and remote, this fantastic upthrust of rock and quartz is near the Tibetan border and about 200 miles northeast from the nearest civilized spot, a town named Kathmandu. Only a handful of Western travelers have seen this shrine. It is reported that the only possible entry is by walking, with the total round-trip hike measuring about 500 miles over precipitous mountain trails. The legend of the mountain states that, over a thousand years ago, a Tibetan master ascetic flew into this spot upon his magic snow lion. He soon realized that this was an unhappy kingdom ruled by a fierce mountain god. The Tibetan master fought and conquered the mountain god. To commemorate the victory, he turned the mountain into a shining pillar of crystal. The people were joyous at being liberated from their cruel master, and ever since that time they have celebrated the event with an annual pilgrimage around the base of the mountain.

This event starts on the day before the full moon in the seventh lunar month. The pilgrims and inhabitants of the area gather at the foot of the mountain in scattered temple buildings. That night, hundreds of tiny fires flicker in the darkness, giving a feeble bit of warmth and comfort to the faithful. Before dawn, everyone is up and on their yearly spiritual journey around the mountain. The way is marked with bleached yak skulls and rows of stone cairns,

as well as fluttering prayer flags placed there by pilgrims. The path
ascends to 16,800 feet as it winds through snowy plateaus.

Occasionally, a pilgrim discovers a rich reward on this journey
by finding a small shaft of quartz crystal. These are called crystal fingers. It is a most meaningful sign, because the crystal is believed to
be more than a symbol; it is an actual generator of divine power to
help the finder. These particular crystals are treasured.

The people call this mountain Shey, the great tent post in the
sky. The word *shey* has been translated from Tibetan to mean crystal
and, also, to perceive or to see clearly. This enormous upthrust from
a primeval sea is almost all rock, rich with marine fossils and scattered throughout with quartz crystals. The area has been described
as being bitterly cold and forsaken but also thoroughly fascinating.
It remains an enchanted land of mysteries.

Shangri La

A hundred seventy-five miles to the south of the "crystal
mountain" is another legendary area, which may be the setting for
Shangri La.

Water is mystically involved in the source of the fictional story
of Shangri La. This tale was created by author James Hilton in his
novel entitled *Lost Horizon*, patterned after the well-known Tibetan
story about Shambhala, a hidden valley of great spiritual significance. As often is the case, these stories have more truth to them
than their readers suspect. Several highly respected authorities say
that they have direct knowledge about Shambhala, that it not only
exists but is currently just as active as it has been for over 4,000
years as a great center for spiritual initiation.

These experts have described the hidden valley as lying in the
shelter of the highest mountain of the world which they call Mount
Cho Mo-Lung-Ma. The English name for this mountain is, of
course, Mount Everest. Shambhala is possibly located on the border between Tibet and Nepal. The sacred valley is deeply wooded
and has many springs and running streams, rich in native rhodo-
dendrons and other magnificent shrubs, trees and flowers. Several
great meadows and a paradisiacal garden are locked in an eternal
deep freeze because they are surrounded by icy mountains. Entry
to this valley is available through a pass on the Nepal side that is
open only at certain times of the year. The rest of the time, the pas-

sage is blocked with ice.

Pilgrims' tales claim that this Shambhala Valley is where the sacred authorities and the spirit of Buddha annually observe the Wesak rites. The Wesak Festival is celebrated worldwide by many millions of followers during the full moon in Taurus, which usually occurs in May. It is a devotional festival in honor of Buddha's first enlightenment, which occurred in a garden under the full moon when Buddha was seated underneath the Bodhi Tree—the Tree of Enlightenment.[3]

The first to arrive for the festival ceremonies are the ecclesiastical officials, who assemble in the guarded upper region of the valley floor. They gather before a long, wide, flat altar which has been carved from a natural outcropping of solid, milky-white quartz.

A round, shallow basin has been carved in the center of this altar; and before the assembled hierarchy, an enormous, round, hollow ball carved from a single piece of clear rock crystal is blessed and fitted securely in the shallow basin of the altar. The crystal globe has a small opening at the top allowing it to be completely filled with pure, sweet water from a nearby sacred ever-flowing spring.

As darkness approaches and the full moon rises, the faithful believe that the spirit of Gautama Buddha descends from above and slowly approaches the water-filled crystal globe. The vital Buddha essence soon merges with the crystal ball of water, saturating it with enlightenment. The Buddha remains thus for some time pouring forth this potent energy, charging the crystal and the water.

After the lengthy ceremonies are complete and the Buddha has ascended again, a portion of the water is removed from the crystal globe and divided among the multitude of pilgrims who have gathered for this observance in the lower part of the valley. The remaining Waters of Enlightenment are carefully guarded and, in some mysterious manner, released to the world in daily proportioned amounts. Some wonder if this event still occurs yearly.

CRYSTALS IN CAMELOT

Crystal plays its symbolic part in the Arthurian legend of Tristan and Isolde where the two sweethearts hide themselves away in a secret cave equipped with a great bed. This is not a lovers' bed for a common rendezvous, but rather a massive, slab-topped structure of solid, icy, quartz crystal. The story tells that the two lovers, fully clothed, stretched themselves out upon the crystal bed. Tristan carefully placed his great sword to lie between him and the fair Isolde as they slept and dreamed together.

Firmly entrenched in the minds of millions of people are fond remembrances from their childhood storybook days. One of the favorites was *The Tales of King Arthur and his Knights of the Round Table.* The mere mention of Camelot could evoke a royal procession of fair maidens protected from evil by their noble knights. King Arthur was always there with Queen Guinevere at his side. Also, there were Sir Gawaine, Sir Lancelot and Sir Galahad forever vanquishing wickedness while upholding the honor and traditions of the Round Table. Fair damsels were swooning and dependent on these valiant men of steel.

The town of Camelot teemed with colorful citizens walking about the streets where brilliant, festive banners were hanging from stone buildings or flying atop poles. What marvelous days those were when knighthood was in flower.

One day I was reading the *Idylls of the King* by Alfred, Lord Tennyson. The opened book spelled out a statement with a revealing clue which held promise of veiled information about crystals. Here is the passage:

And there I saw mage Merlin, whose vast wit
And hundred winters are but as the hands
Of loyal vassals toiling for their liege.
And near him stood the Lady of the Lake,
Who knows a subtler magic than his own—
Clothed in white samite, mystic, wonderful.
She gave the king his huge, cross-hilted sword,
Whereby to drive the heathen out; a mist
Of incense curl'd about her, and her face
Well nigh was hidden in the minster gloom;
But there was heard among the holy hymns
A voice as of the waters, for she dwells
Down in the deep; calm, whatsoever storms
May shake the world, and when the surface rolls
Hath power to walk the waters like our Lord.

To me, this passage clearly indicates that the Lady of the Lake was far more ingenious and enlightened than the king's magician,

Merlin. Since Lord Tennyson was a great Arthurian scholar, he knew that Merlin obviously had a rival that surpassed him.

Inasmuch as the Lady reputedly lived comfortably under the waters of the lake as well as walking upon its surface, she was surely a water goddess. It is therefore probable that she was adept at using crystals to increase her powers.

Who could suspect the stories of King Arthur would be anything but fantasy? The clue about the Lady of the Lake did seem to have some merit, so an investigation was started. After much literary searching and some extremely valuable interviews with visiting British Arthurian experts, a much different version of the days of King Arthur gradually unfolded.

Scholars believe the legends were actually based on historical figures, as well as certain geographical places which still exist. The real King Arthur is thought to have been born in Cornwall about 500 A.D. when he was sired by King Uther Pendragon.

It was known that King Uther became enamored with Lady Igerna, who was the Duchess of Cornwall. The duke and duchess frequently attended the king's court. It was whispered that Uther was able to gain frequent access to Lady Igerna's bedchambers through the courtesy of a magic spell cast by Merlin.

With a few passes of the hand accompanied by a muttered incantation, Merlin bewitched the king so he looked exactly like Lady Igerna's husband, the duke. Eventually her ladyship gave birth to their son who was named Arthur. Upon the death of the monarch, Arthur ascended the throne although he was still in his early youth.

After being crowned King of Brittany, he formed the Knights of the Round Table and soon became their war chieftain. He led them into battle after battle, always victorious. When the noble knights were not out fighting, they were spending their hours at Camelot jousting and pursuing the gentle maidens of the town. According to medieval songs and historical notations, Camelot thrived as a center for gallant knights and beauteous damsels pursuing amorous adventures and dangerous intrigues.

During the long days at court, King Arthur became enamored of King Lot's wife, who also happened to be his half sister. He called on Merlin for a love potion, which must have worked because it enabled the king to carry on his incestuous affair in the castle. As a result of this dalliance, his son Mordred was born. Many years later when Mordred was a grown man and King Arthur happened to be away on one of his wars, Mordred chose this opportunity to temporarily crown himself King of Brittany and then proceeded to pursue Queen Guinevere down the hallways and through the bedrooms of the castle, but without success.

At another time, Sir Lancelot became enchanted with the charms of the Queen. It seems she found Sir Lancelot's attentions pleasing, so she warmly enticed him, thus encouraging new gossip in the castle. The shadowy figure of Merlin was interwoven with many of these day and night activities. He always seemed ready to aid an aspiring lover. The magician was reputedly neither good or evil; his powers were made readily available and could be used for either purpose as needed. Merlin's reputation was that of a great spellcaster. It seems, however, that he was just as well known as a court entertainer. He devoted endless hours performing for the court at Camelot as a bard, and he was popularly known as the singing sage.

In those days, the news was spread throughout the kingdom by singing bards reciting and rhyming the feats of the day. Many sources of information state that the bards were an organized guild of male entertainers. Their membership was often hereditary and closed to outsiders. Rarely, if ever, was there mention of a female bard. As was the custom, the guild functioned at the court through the courtesy of the king. There exists the possibility that this arrangement could explain the abundance of stories about the magical abilities of Merlin while almost completely ignoring the astounding deeds of the Lady of the Lake, King Arthur's neighbor.

Much of Merlin's reputation came from the claim that he mysteriously transported many huge rocks from Ireland and assembled them in a magical formation on the Salisbury plain. Today, this collection of giant stones is known as Stonehenge.

Merlin's transportation of Stonehenge from Ireland to Salisbury must be the most heroic and potent magic in all history, as Stonehenge was completely finished about 2,000 years before Merlin was born!

Lady Vivian ruled over her own enchanted kingdom composed of a vast lake with an island having a great crystal mountain rising upwards to the clouds. Her castle was built on the side of this crystal mountain where she was said to be tended by 10,000 handmaidens.

Vivian had complete control over the waters of her lake. When Arthur desperately needed strength, she brought forth a mystical arm which rose from the depths of the lake, raising the great sword Excalibur above the waters for the king to take. Arthur seated himself in a small boat and Merlin rowed him to the outstretched arm waiting for him. King Arthur seized the sword and brandished it, instantly realizing the rush of power bestowed on him by the wonders of the Lady of the Lake.

Years later in the twilight days of the court, the king's head was dreadfully wounded from a traitorous blow struck by his evil son, Mordred. With great concern, Arthur ordered his loyal knight, Sir Bedivere, to take the magic sword Excalibur and fling it back into the lake for safekeeping. Sir Bedivere threw the great sword far outward from the shore, where it was caught in midair by the mystical arm that suddenly arose from the waters. The arm shook Excalibur three times in salute to the king, then slowly sank into the depths.

When the stories of Merlin's magic reached the Lady of the Lake, she was curious and decided to meet him. She chose the enchanted fountain at Barenton for their meeting place. The waters of the fountain had miraculous powers that healed and strengthened; and, of course, it was Vivian who controlled these wonders. She blew a spell into the air which caused Merlin to visit the fountain and stand there gazing at the flowing waters. Vivian walked slowly by him and smiled as she passed. He instantly became intoxicated with her charms and followed her. She led him to the nearby Garden of Joys and, before night had ended, had seduced him and put him completely under her control.

She soon made Merlin her willing prisoner; she led him to a magic cell where she taught him many secrets. This cell has been described as a large cavern lined with sparkling crystals—a crystal cave.

The abilities of this lady seemed to be beneficent. Under her rule, her kingdom prospered and overflowed with peace, love, and joy. Her castle on the side of the crystal mountain had many rooms—more than enough for the 10,000 handmaidens. She was surrounded by a paradise of green plants with ever-bearing fresh fruit throughout the year. The flowers continuously blossomed, filling the air with sweet perfume.

It was on this spellbinding island that Sir Lancelot spent his childhood days. Tales are told that he was either deserted by his mother, or Vivian spirited him away. In either case, Vivian took the infant to her island kingdom where he was raised in the midst of luxury. When he came to the age of manhood, Vivian took him to King Arthur's court nearby and had him knighted.

Like Moses of Biblical fame, Lancelot was found as a tiny babe, raised in royal surroundings and eventually became a great leader.

From these stories, it is evident Vivian had powers greatly different from those of Merlin. She carefully bestowed loving magic; sowing benevolent miracles that could be fruitful. The lady was a creative enchantress. In comparison, Merlin was indiscriminate with a tawdry type of magic.

Since the Lady of the Lake was a water goddess, she was as much at home on the bottom of the lake as she was in her castle. We wonder what treasures besides Excalibur were stored in the depths of her watery kingdom. Her upper abode, the castle built on the slopes of the crystal mountain, again stressed the association of crystal with magic and flowing water. The symbols of Vivian's kingdom are in marked contrast to the mighty war-like atmosphere of King Arthur. The Lady had the calmness of her lake, the mysteries of its depths, the serenity of her mountain, and the peace of her island paradise.

As we can see, she has given us an example of an enchanted life with a meaningful message. Magic is not and should not be confused with evil. Magic is power, an energy that can produce marvelous things. Evil is the misuse of this power. Real magic is the creative use of the human mind in honorable and benevolent pursuits.

Before we leave the Lady of the Lake, there is the question of why her historical virtues have been widely neglected. The character Merlin is promoted and praised in glowing terms in hundreds of stories, while Lady Vivian has long been relegated to the shadows. Could there be a similarity between her fate and the Virgin Mary who is so infrequently mentioned in the Bible? After all, Mary was the mother of the Savior Jesus. Conversely the bad girl Mary Magdalene was given a great deal of attention, being mentioned many times in comparison to the mother of Jesus.

Historical scholars tell me that there may be a reason. It seems that the entire history of the world has been recorded by males for the glory of and consumption by males. Practically all historians were men, because females were not usually allowed to learn to read or write. In addition, the historians were privileged to function as long as their product was pleasing to the ruling class. This weaving of tales through a political maze of threats, promises and retributions, as well as the occasional burning of libraries, gives rise to enormous doubts that anyone really knows the true history of the human race.

NOTES

1. The symbolism is, of course, the white Christ light to "show the way."

2. Black and white "fortune" stones were in common use as omens to foretell lucky and unlucky days, as well as favorable and unfavorable ventures and condemnation or acquittal at trials. See the Latin word *lapillus*.

3. The Bodhi Tree is a fig tree, *Ficus religiosa,* also called the Bo-Tree and the Peepul tree—a large upright tree with delicate foliage of thin, pale-green leaves that tremble in the slightest breeze, giving an overall fluttering effect.

Crystal Facts

Holy Ice is a book about crystals—not just any crystals, but real electronic quartz crystals. Electronic crystal is that flawless form of crystal which is used in countless electrical components. Most naturally occurring quartz crystal is not electronic; only a small percentage of high quality material will perform. It is the high quality crystal that was mankind's first solid state device.

In ancient times the crystals were shaped by craftsmen into working crystals which resembled semi-round balls and talisman symbols such as moons, crosses and the like. These working crystals were in daily use for healing purposes as well as for protection and survival.

THE SUBCONSCIOUS

It was explained that each newborn human comes equipped with a built-in subconscious commander. This invisible dictator controls heartbeats, blood pressure, digestion, breathing and other physical activities that keep life functioning. The genes that govern hair color, eye color, skin type, body style and other physical traits also carry another parcel of enforcements. These direct individual patterns of likes and dislikes, talents and faults, and spontaneous reactions. To a marked degree, every being is preprogrammed for

101

his or her activities in this world by his or her ancestry, both near and remote. Those who fail to understand such things are automatically influenced to serve their life as a slave to their hidden genetic master.

Those individuals who do comprehend this and realize who they are understand the importance of taking control of their subconscious yearnings and desires, their loves and hates and especially their automatic responses. To the enlightened, the crystal and its ability to amplify signals coursing through the electronic communications system of the body help make the task easier.

A crystal working tool boosts the ability of the mind to contact and communicate with the subconscious.

This can go further because the superconscious and universal consciousness can also be brought into this same network of communications.

It is also believed that certain spiritually advanced souls can understand and practice crystal-aided meditation so they can bridge the mystical chasm all the way to the meta-conscious while remaining physically alive in their limited five sense body.

(The meta-conscious is above and beyond all consciousness as understood by the mind. This is believed to be a state of complete purity of the absolute.)

The Role of the Hypothalamus

The hypothalamus is found in what may be the most protected spot in the skull. It lies under the thalamus, which is situated beneath the left and right brain in almost the center of the head. The hypothalamus serves as the telephone switchboard for the entire body. It monitors all vital signs and orders any necessary corrective measures to keep the system running smoothly. It governs the basic human drives of hunger, thirst and sex, and is responsible for broadcasting signals of fear and anger. It contains neurosecretions which aid in the control of metabolic activities. It regulates the body temperatures and their swings, and it controls the secretions of the endocrine glands.

The hypothalamus is the main subcortical area for the control of the sympathetic and parasympathetic nervous system.

The pituitary gland is directly beneath and connected to the hypothalamus. The hypothalamus sends its messages to the pitu-

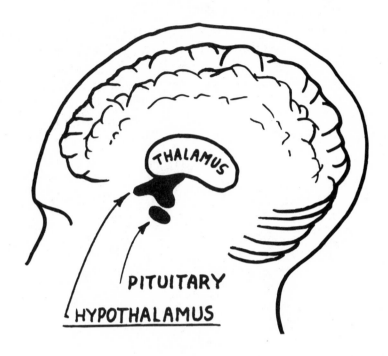

Location of the Hypothalamus

itary, which controls hormones, general metabolism, chemical balance, blood pressure, body-fluid levels, ovulation and sexual desires.

Control messages are sent throughout the body by both electrical and chemical activities. The release of chemicals by neurons aids in the electrical transmission from one cell to another.

The hypothalamus is an essential gland and is possibly influenced by the tiniest electronic impulse. The hypothalamus contains within itself a complex switchboard network to send messages throughout the entire body system and the brain. We know that it is stimulated by exterior vibrations received through the five senses. The hypothalamus also receives oscillation energies radiated by electronic quartz crystals.

By exposing the subconscious mind to pure vibrations, the subconscious can be influenced to balance body chemistry, to heal and to achieve new goals, as well as change old ways. Whatever the vibrational message may be, the hypothalamus is believed to receive these impulses and send them throughout the body.

This, then, is one of the secrets of ages past from our mystical forefathers who stuck a tiny piece of quartz crystal on the end of a stick and made it into a magic wand. The wand was employed to gain divine guidance for major decisions of great weight. In use, the quartz crystal sent a signal via the body cells into the hypothalamus and out through the nervous system until it finally developed into full consciousness. Then they knew that they knew.

ELECTRONIC QUARTZ CRYSTAL

A live electronic crystal was born many millions of years ago deep in the earth from the forces of fire and water. The ancients called it "Holy Ice" and said it was frozen holy water spilled out of heaven.

To most people, this particular type of crystal is merely a chunk of common quartz; to the initiated, it is an original solid-state device—a natural semi-conductor, amplifying reflector, an advantageous tool for victory and survival.

The ancients secretly reserved the crystal for use by the religious hierarchy, royalty, military leaders and, of course, the secret brotherhoods. Crystals were used as natural amplifiers to cultivate the mind and sharpen the instincts and intuition. Today, the high living standards enjoyed are largely due to electronic communications. The telephone, radio, television, computers and many other communication devices function because of their ability to separate and isolate selected wavelengths so they can be put to practical use.

One single item has pioneered this modern miracle and that is a product of Mother Nature—the electronic quartz crystal.

If the crystal and all knowledge derived from it were obliterated, the world would be plunged backwards into the dark ages of isolation.

Electronic Quartz Crystals Versus Natural Crystal Points

The natural quartz crystal point as found in the ground has been widely touted as the supreme crystal. Dozens upon dozens of books have been published with claims of great and almost magical results happening from crystal-point usage.

It is undoubtedly true that sensible use of a good working crystal can result in many benefits. It is unfortunate that the natural crystal point with its six flat sides converging to a pointed, pyramid-shaped top is simply not efficient for metaphysical or psychic use. A crystal, like a radio receiver, must be turned on to use it. It must be activated by a source of electrical energy. A crystal user can turn on a crystal by wearing it next to the body or better yet by grasping it in the hand.

By wrapping the fingers around a crystal, it starts reacting to energies received from the living cells and the mental output of the brain. The crystal then starts vibrating on a frequency compatible and in harmony with the body and the brain. Upon receiving pulsed messages from its energy source, the crystal then amplifies and broadcasts them outward in spiral waves of energy information. Electronic engineers have called this an amplifying reflector.

If the crystal is efficient, these messages may be received by the body cells, the subconscious and the conscious mind of a good crystal user. Much of this may be subliminal and received mostly by the subconscious and body cells, which may or may not relay it on the five-sense mind. A knowledgeable crystal user can usually get the subconscious to cooperate and deliver the information.

Let us take a mental journey into the center of a crystal point and carefully look around. We find ourselves in a hall of mirrors with six flat sides ascending up to a point. This creates an array of dazzling reflections reflecting and re-reflecting countless shadows and lights from the mirrors. Let us now suppose the crystal is being activated. As it receives the outside energies, we would see a rotating spiral ball of electronic forces which would grow and fill the inside. These spiral waves would then start hitting against the flat sides where they would ricochet to another flat surface and then another again, and again and again. Most of these energies are being dissipated and shattered into thousands of weak, ghost images. The outward escaped broadcasts are very weak and often garbled.

Many thousands of years ago crystal workers found that river-tossed quartz crystals eventually became rounded much like cobblestones. This is how the first crystal balls came into existence. The crystal workers soon found that the river-tossed quartz balls were much more active than the crystal points that they had been using. When some of the balls were polished, they discovered that the activity was again greatly increased. From that time on the initiates would use only the rounded and polished crystal pieces.

In the early 1970s it was noted that, when a concave surface of a crystal met a convex surface (much like the letter S), the broadcast strength was often increased. This was noted by many people who saw the famed crystal skull in San Francisco. Most of them could feel more activity coming from the crystal skull where the concave eye sockets would meet the convex surfaces of the forehead and cheek bones.

The single crystal point is beautiful indeed. Its shiny, mirror-like, flat surfaces reflect the light of the five-sense world in myriad patterns. It has many valuable uses, and it may well have been the original inspiration for the science of faceting gemstones to increase their glitter. The single crystal point's best usage lies in the physical world.

On the other hand, for usage in mind control and development plus achievements both physical and mental, the crystal with carved, rounded and polished surfaces is the one that really does the work. Its response to mental activities is remarkable.

CLEAR AND COLORED CRYSTALS

The finest transparent gem grade of pure quartz crystal is inherently colorless, and most pieces discovered have this characteristic, but they are also commonly found in innumerable shades of smoky, yellow, amethyst, and rose colors. Whenever this occurs it means that an impurity has found its way into the quartz structure.

Smoky quartz is caused by tiny traces of aluminum present in the crystal. If the crystal has grown in a spot where there was absolutely no natural radiation of any strength it would be clear, rock crystal. However, if the growth area had deposits of radioactive ore such as uranium, the gamma radiation present would color the crystal and make it a "smoky."

The smoky colors range from a very pale smoke to practically coal black, depending on the amount of radiation, length of exposure time and quantity of the aluminum impurity. In addition, the color may be a very warm smoke or a cold tone smoke.

When a crystal has traces of ferric iron instead of aluminum and has also been subjected to irradiation, the resulting color could be many shades of yellow, orange or amethyst. Some crystals are citrine yellow on one end and amethyst on the other. Rockhounds have dubbed them ametrine. The change of color from amethyst to citrine was caused by a change of the location of the ferric iron

River Tumbled Crystal and Lopsided Crystal Ball

impurity from one end of the crystal to the other. Every quartz crystal structure contains within itself a color center. When the ferric iron impurity is located in a certain spot in the color center, the crystal is colored amethyst. If it is located in a different position, the color is citrine.

It should be noted that heat treating colored crystals can either change the color or in some cases completely eliminate it. Certain grades of amethyst (not the highest quality) are commercially heat treated which changes the color from amethyst to yellow brown, brownish orange, or "topaz" color. If the results are not satisfactory, the amethyst color can be restored by bombarding the heat treated crystals with gamma waves.

Rose and amethyst crystals have an exceptionally wide range of both color and quality. The rare ones are perfectly transparent, with an even coloring of clean rose or deep royal amethyst, while thousands of tons of lesser quality contain chemical impurities of many types, which are undesirable for electronics as well as marring the color purity of the crystal.

The new process of recycling small and broken quartz crystals into larger perfect ones makes it possible to grow the finest gem-quality crystals in almost any color desired. In addition, the colors may be better and more permanent than normally found in nature.

Only one major type of quartz crystal so far has not been successfully grown, and that is the angel's hair or rutilated crystal. Angel's hair gets its name from its fascinating appearance. Slender needles of rutile, or titanium dioxide, sometimes grow in cavities in the earth. These hollow spots are later filled with new crystal growth, thus imprisoning the rutile in solid quartz crystal. This results in sparkling chunks of clear, transparent crystal shot through with glistening, tiny hair-like strands of rutile appearing as blonde or silver baby hair.

THE SEA OF ELECTRONIC ENERGY

The human race lives in a vast sea of electromagnetic energy waves. Every individual is constantly saturated with direct and stray beams of both manmade and natural rays. The major portion of this active matter is generated from various mineral deposits in the earth's crust and from celestial sources far outside of mankind's control.

One example is sunlight which is composed of a complex range of various radiant energies. Out of this wide spectrum beamed toward the earth, humans are conscious of only two parts: the infrared, which gives warmth, and the visible light, which enables sight. The rest is generally ignored because the magnificent sensing apparatus of the physical body receives, but does not seem to relay information of this nature to the five sense conscious mind.

A DEMONSTRATION BY THOMAS EDISON

I found some notes in the library about a talk given by Thomas Edison to the National Academy of Sciences which went something like this. Edison stood before his scientist friends. In front of him was a bronze statue of a beautiful maiden.

"Gentlemen," he said, "I want to illustrate a few of the different vibrations we should learn to understand. I have a little black box, a secret little box placed at the base of this bronze statue, and I will set the control dial to hold the vibration at 16 cycles per second."

No one heard or felt or sensed any change; however, all of the termites actively tried to leave the building because their sensory mechanism warned them of an unnatural and perhaps hostile condition developing.

Edison adjusted the control to increase the vibration to 32 cycles per second. All of the scientists smiled and nodded to each other. There was a low rumbling and all of them could sense it, feel it, and hear it.

Edison said, "That's fine. Let's turn it up some more." So he adjusted the control to around 6,000 cycles, and everyone heard that. It was very loud, a piercing harmonic note. Then he advanced the control to 16,000 cycles, and none of the male scientists heard or sensed anything at all.

Then Edison explained, "You don't detect this energy; however, it is smoothly vibrating at 16,000 cycles. Let me turn it up some more."

But they couldn't feel any difference.

"I am turning it higher," he said, and the bronze statue started to glow a dull red color that could both be seen and felt.

"Aha," he said. "At a very high frequency, it is giving off heat. I will advance it again."

The bronze statue gleamed incandescent white. There was no trouble in sensing the light and the heat. He turned the dial to a vastly higher frequency, and the bronze statue flashed one puff and vanished. It went into such a high vibration that it was no longer reacting to the normal laws of gravity and space.

"It is not earthbound anymore," Edison said.

It was explained that, when the control box reduced the vibration back to normal, the statue would reappear physically. Where it might materialize would depend upon gravity, space, and time. It could reappear in Asia, Africa or Australia. This editorialized version[1] of Edison's address before the Academy of Sciences is an example of the type of phenomena we were researching to clarify the energies of the crystal skull. Our own studies carried us ever further into additional fascinating discoveries.

SILICA

Glass is commonly made by fusing good silica sand along with soda ash and a few other ingredients. Glass solidifies from its molten state without crystallization taking place. Science regards glass as a supercooled liquid rather than a true solid. That is why glass is called amorphous, which means it does not have a crystalline structure. Glass is simply a liquid that turned solid on cooling.

As far as electronics is concerned, glass is regarded as an insulator.

Originally glass was undoubtedly created as imitation crystal because big chunks of solid, flawless quartz crystal were exceedingly rare. Quartz crystal, unlike glass, has a three-dimensional network structure. The cells of the network are symmetrical and repeatable. As the crystal grows larger in size it keeps repeating this symmetrical structure again and again. If it is a single, untwinned crystal of high quality without impurities or flaws it would normally be an electronic crystal. The impurities found in high quality colored crystals such as smoky, citrine and amethyst are so minute and undetectable they usually would not interfere in any way with the electronic capabilities. The amount of aluminum impurity in a good smoky crystal could be from 18 to 25 parts per million.

Indeed, more than one electronic engineer has entertained the thought that perhaps the slight impurity and radiation treatment could even stabilize the crystal and slightly increase its electronic abilities.

"Lead crystal" is a type of glass used for thousands of years to imitate gemstones of all nature, because of its coloring properties. Red or green causes the substance to resemble rubies or emeralds; other tints are also available. Lead crystal is very shiny, bright and sparkling. Because of the high lead content, lead crystal is very easy to cut and polish. Basically, it is very soft glass. Common lead crystal is 50 per cent silica and 30 per cent lead oxide, plus the usual traces of soda and other trace minerals. Manufacturing lead crystal is a tremendous industry, but we must not confuse the words "lead crystal" with the words "quartz crystal" because they are different. Lead crystal is glass and is composed of a manufactured product. Quartz crystal grows in the ground. It is a product of Mother Nature.

What happens to quartz crystal when heated high enough to melt? At three different temperatures interesting changes are worth noting because the crystal changes twice before finally melting. The first change takes place at 867 degrees centigrade. Here, the crystal changes into a substance called *tridymite*. At a higher temperature of 1470 degrees centigrade, this tridymite will change into another silica-based substance called *cristobalite*, a white chalky material used to make silica brick valued for use in the refractory linings of high-melting-point furnaces necessary for the steel and the glass industries. The further application of heat resulting in temperatures above 1,710 degrees centigrade causes the silica to finally melt to a liquid.

Upon cooling, this molten silica becomes a glass which is commonly called "fused quartz." To label this glass as quartz crystal is both incorrect and misleading, because once the crystal is melted to a liquid, it become amorphous and loses any crystalline structure or crystal characteristics. This is important to remember because there are many commercially made articles represented as being pure quartz crystal when they are really silica glass. Silica glass is easily molded, stamped and machine mass produced into many forms. On the other hand, raw crystal requires carving, sanding and polishing. Traditionally, a skilled craftsman called a crystal cutter accomplishes this handiwork.

PSYCHIC TOOLS

Crystal objects such as crystal talismans, necklaces, bracelets, crowns, altar pieces, palm-working crystals and crystal balls are all working psychic tools. These crystals were more than mere badges of authority or symbols of power for royalty. They helped to increase and heighten the instincts of the rulers. This greatly aided them to stay in power. Crystals were necessary tools for survival. I believe that the adornment function of these gems was strictly a by-product that came into play when the wealthy commoners used various colored stones in what they thought to be the same manner. They made ornaments out of all different kinds of colored stones and, thus, the jewelry trade was born in imitation of the crystal psychic tools of royalty and religious leaders.

Today, quartz crystal is the mineral symbol for this Age of Communications we are just entering. The gathering of data proves that this is indeed the Crystal Age. Anyone can thumb through any magazine and see the different items now controlled by quartz crystals. The oscillating quartz crystal and the working knowledge derived from it has dramatically raised the living standards in the incredibly short time of less than a century. All of our modern communications systems—radio, television, telephone and all the rest—are possible due to this new knowledge of wavelength separation and control of oscillation and digital pulsing. Without these communications, we would be truly set back to the dark ages.

The most sophisticated and advanced electronic equipment today, including the computer, is made possible through the advancement of our knowledge derived from electronic crystals. However, all modern miracles are minuscule in their content as compared to the abilities of the human mind, which is capable of freeing the physical body from the majority of disease and pain through application of control. When accidents and inescapable diseases do strike, the human mind is capable of speeding up the time needed for the healing process, reducing months and weeks into days and hours.

Modern scientists have experimented with lasers and quartz crystals, adapting them as a permanent memory bank of factual data to be safely stored away inside a crystal and recovered at a later date on command. Studies indicate this use was preceded for untold ages by priests who used crystals to store blessings and curses.

Crystal is a natural storehouse for preserving data. The crystal is believed to be capable of storing mental thoughts and directions in vibrational form which repeats much like a continuously play-ing tape recorder. Since crystal is a permanent material which nei-ther ages nor decays, how long would the data fed into a crystal last? Could it remain active for thousands of years? If so, this could easily explain ancient curses such as King Tut's curse.

We have heard from British archaeologists and scholars that crystal objects were buried in tombs for this purpose. The crystals were programmed in a ceremony with instructions to protect the contents from vandals and robbers and to destroy and punish any-one who violated the tomb. The secret crystal was usually hidden in the west wall.[2] If this crystal object were found and touched by someone who violated the sanctity of that tomb, and if their sub-conscious mind were capable of understanding the instructions given in an ancient language, the curse could work. The ancient intent would have the same effect as any modern black magic curse which orders the subconscious mind to cooperate and pun-ish the individual in which it is staying. To understand that a crys-tal could be used as a curse that lasted for thousands of years helps one to understand that it could also be used to help others—an important understanding.

The Mitchell-Hedges crystal skull is one of the most important

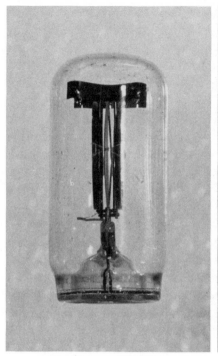 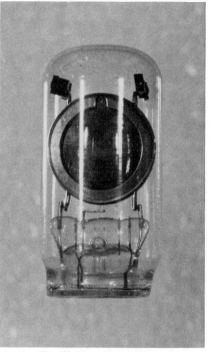

Oscillator—Side View	*Oscillator—Front View*
Crystal is center sliced between two metal guard rings, crosstie wires in center hold crystal in place.	*Crystal is suspended between two visible metal guard rings so it can oscillate freely.*

artifacts found to date because it bears a message from our ancestors. The mind is unquestionably the greatest thing in the Universe, simultaneously the most wondrous and the most fearsome, like two sides of a coin, like the yin and the yang, the daylight and the darkness. The mind is not the brain; the brain is a portion of the body. The mind is of the spirit and substance. It is a part of the Creator set free. The mind has the greatest gift of all—the gift of freedom of choice.

CATOPTROMANCY

Mirrors are classical divining instruments, and the first portable mirror was likely a flawed piece of quartz crystal. Mirror divination is called *catoptromancy*. Older, unabridged dictionaries, including some published as late as the 1930s, define a mirror as a crystal used by diviners. The literal translation of the word "mirror" from its

Arabic and Latin roots means to marvel and to wonder.

The earliest written records about mirrors came from the Etruscans, Greeks and Romans. Pliny mentioned mirrors of glass coated with tin or silver; however, most mirrors were metal discs polished on one side. Later in the 13th century, Venetian glass mirrors became very popular.

A few examples of mirrors as magical devices for divining are the all-seeing mirrors in the Arabian Nights and Vulcan's mirror which told the past, present and the future. Chaucer's Canterbury Tales intrigued its readers with a magical mirror that gave warnings of future disasters. Snow White's wicked stepmother consulted the magic mirror on the wall, and Alice went right through her magic looking glass and discovered a world in reverse.

Going beyond hand-held objects, the very first mirror might have been a reflecting pool of water in which our long-ago ancestors saw their images. Still, the first portable mirror might have been a chunk of rock crystal—not any rock crystal, but a special piece that had a shiny, natural mirror locked within itself. Such pieces do exist, and certain ones have been highly prized by medicine men.

Even though quartz crystal is formed and often remains buried deep underground, a perfectly clear, transparent crystal may be cracked. With the proper conditions and time, the crystal will grow much larger and "heal" itself. This leaves an inside crack which looks like a bright, reflective mirror embedded in clear crystal. If a tiny amount of natural oil and moisture had penetrated into the crack before it sealed itself, it would have created a shine. This made a micro-thin coating that changed the refractive index, thus reflecting large amounts of light rather than transmitting it. Here was a real treasure to any wonderworker who found it—a solid chunk of God-sent Holy Water with a magic mirror locked inside it!

In these modern times, such a piece of crystal, except for a rare display specimen, would usually be tossed aside into the scrap bin. The comment might be, "It's just a chunk of cracked quartz. Who likes flaws?"

The conscious five-sense mind has expressed itself; however, the sight of the magic mirror may have stirred some action in the subconscious memory bank where long-unused recollections have been stored. Some of this energy could flow into consciousness without being understood. If so, the individual might have felt an uneasy, nagging suspicion that somehow, something or other has gone wrong.

THE HUMAN BODY IS A SUPER ANTENNA

Mother Nature has equipped the human body with three of four essential components of a fine radio receiving system. The necessary four components are the antenna, the tuner, the amplifier and the reproduction system, which, in a radio, are the speakers.

The body with its complex electrical network of nerves and high moisture content is a sensitive antenna system capable of receiving signals from an uncountable variety of sources. The human mind may be the most selective tuning system known. The brain (which is not the mind) is an admirable reproduction system which can then employ the five senses to interpret received signals.

The single missing component is the amplifier, which is needed to boost signal strength. Ancient man discovered that quartz crystal boosted vague intuitions out of the dim mists into reality that sometimes could be seen, heard, felt, smelled and tasted.

Crystal practitioners believe that the use of good working crystals can be of great value in helping human needs to amplify the communications systems within. This seems to be especially true to those seeking intuitive creativity. The crystal excels in making conscious many things an individual already knows and is capable of accomplishing while not consciously aware of this untapped knowledge.

On the cellular level, crystal amplification is believed to encourage maximum cell consciousness and communications, which strengthens the link from the lowest cell level up to the subconscious mind and the subconscious memory bank. The communication system is believed to continue its connection onward to the five-sense conscious mind, thus eventually enabling control of the subconscious commands by the conscious mind.

This is not the final stopping point for this complex communications network. The route is further believed to continue upward from the conscious to the superconscious mind. The final link connects the superconscious to the metaconscious source, which is absolute purity, above and beyond all things.

This amazing electronic communications network within every human is one reason why prayers get results. As an example, visualize one or more persons intelligently sending out prayers for an ill friend far away. Said sincerely and coherently with purpose, these prayers are seriously projected with strength.

The cellular level communications system is in some mysterious manner able to forward the message across the miles to the right recipient. The ill person may or may not consciously realize these signals even while their body cells clearly get the message. No doubt exists that the body cells can vigorously respond to prayer stimulation. The immune system is reactivated and the body chemistry rebalanced for the better. This can be repeated with good results.

Scientists tell us that the world itself was created about four and a half billion years ago; and man, according to our anthropologists, has been on this earth as the species *Homo sapiens* for not more than 100,000 to 500,000 years at most. But erect-walking ancestors of *Homo sapiens* are traced back about three and a half to four million years earlier. Dated fossil skulls from 500,000 years ago seem to indicate that there was a sudden, very large increase in the size and capacity of the brain box at this time. According to scientists, the stage was then set for the introduction of *Homo sapiens*.

If we will accept that man has been on earth in his present form for a least 300,000 years, we must also understand that his subconscious memory bank has stored relevant, genetic information dating back for approximately this same length of time. Very simply put, the fertilized cell from which the individual developed carries genetic memory codes of instructions. These cells determine inherited traits such as skin and hair color, bone structure, and other physical characteristics of the body.

Far more important to our lives is the subconscious memory behind memorable happenings and reactions that are also included in this genetic code. This indicates that man is instinctively reacting and playing out his life in accordance with signals sent out through the nervous system signals influenced by over 300,000 years of genetic memories.

PROGRAMMING

Those not aware of their subconscious programming can never be free to have full control of their thoughts, their reactions and their lives by their conscious mind because their reactions, moods, patterns, habits and goals of fulfillment are vitally fed to them by their subconscious commander, who simply relays this information from their genetic memory bank.

They are programmed with influences fed into their system from the indelible features of 300,000 years of survival, as well as the programming that has been given to them by their parents, relatives, teachers and associates since their inception into the human body. So in order to be enlightened, it is necessary to be free to control and reprogram the impulses from the subconscious (which contains the genetic memory bank) rather than to respond to them blindly.

Natural quartz crystal is believed to have been in use during the last 12,000 to 15,000 years by a great many of our leaders for this and other purposes.

When the crystal is programmed, it is saturated with the given instruction and the whole person receives the same treatment. The crystal amplifies and relays these given vibrations into the cells of the body, which receive and record them for future use. Let us carefully examine these processes another way. The scientist today will tell us that light—either colored or clear light—enters the cells of the body through the auditory nerves. In like manner, the vibrations from a crystal are transmitted through electrical impulse to the body cells and the brain. Light, as an example, when entering the body cells, stimulates the pineal gland which then produces mellantonin, a powerful neuro-humoral agent necessary for the proper functioning of the brain.

The hypothalamus functions as the switchboard network of the brain and directing the moment-to-moment vital processes of the body. Practically everything that goes on in the body is directed through this network—blood pressure, breathing, digestion, and the fact that your heart continues to beat when you go to sleep at night. You don't have to think to keep breathing or to keep your heart beating, or to have your digestion take care of that dinner that you enjoyed hours earlier.

The hypothalamus is thought to direct all of these vital processes through its telephone-like switchboard network by its direct and intermediate connections to the pituitary gland and the autonomic nervous system. These messages feed into the parasympathetic and sympathetic nervous system which control the blood flow and body's oxygenation processes.

So, by exposing the subconscious mind to pure vibration, be it light, sound, or whatever, and by subjecting the subconscious mind to this stimulation, it is possible to reprogram the body cells and balance the neuro-endocrine system of the body.

When mentally and verbally programming a crystal, the intent and belief of the individual is every bit as important as the content. The subconscious memory bank, which at an age of 300,000 years or more, cannot be tricked by human beings who play games with their very limited, five-sense minds. Anything that has lived as long as 300,000 years must be a veteran of innumerable deceits.

When you mentally and verbally program a crystal, the intent and belief is of prime importance. If the conscious act of the individual is not fully sincere, this can be instantly detected by the subconscious, and the content of the message could be cancelled out as worthless or diverted into a different meaning selected as being more suitable. In other words, the subconscious takes command and starts to rule again as before.

However, if the individual is sincere, has faith and strong motivation for success, the subconscious is believed to accept these new directions. Thus, the entire system of the body may rebalance itself in adjustment to new instructions.

Programming a crystal is best accomplished by holding it in the right hand—the giving hand—and resting the right hand in the left so as to make good contact. The left hand thus receives all the crystal-amplified signals from the right, hand-held crystal and relays them up the left arm into the reception centers of the brain. The signals are routed through the hypothalamus switchboard network and sent up into the brain and out to the body's cells and glands and down the right arm to the right hand. After completing this circuit, the crystal then receives the same signals sent out and reamplifies and rebroadcasts them to be replayed in the same closed-loop circuit.

Feeding in Information

The information is fed into the crystal by talking to it out loud. Sound plus skin contact does the job. Raising the voice is not necessary; a normal tone is sufficient.

The crystal should be regarded as an electronic tool, compared to a microphone which receives sound-wave energy and converts it to electromagnetics and sends it on. Nothing would be accomplished by holding a microphone and directing mental thoughts.

Of course, the crystal has no understanding of its own. Like a microphone, the crystal is merely a responsive electronic device which reacts to energy and vibrations. A crystal is no philosopher nor a thinking being, but it does respond. When thoughts are assembled and formed into words and logical sentences, then relayed out into the airwaves via the vocal cords, a great deal more mental and physical energy is expended than by silently thinking. More brain cells and additional body cells are activated and the message, in almost all cases, is very much clearer because of this extra effort.

While the crystal may not understand the implications of the vibrations passing through it, from both the hand and the voice, the body and brain cells receiving them most undoubtedly do. The mind and the physical body take a part in sending out these particular vibrations, so when the signals are received back from the crystal, a complete understanding of the translation of these identical vibrations back into thoughtful meanings is possible.

The crystal continues repeating these signals for an indefinite time into the future. If at any time a wish to change the programming is present, one may simply erase past vibrations by holding the crystal in full sunlight and programming it to wipe itself clear. Why this works is not clearly understood, but it is believed that, since ultraviolet rays pass easily and completely through real electronic quartz crystal, they aid in flushing out the previously energized vibrations. The crystal may be compared to a tape recorder with a superior quality erasable tape that may be reused.

CRYSTAL IN THE COMMUNICATIONS AGE

With good reason, crystals have been called the magical servants of the space age, for they have made this age possible. The simple quartz crystal has been in use for much more than 12,000 years in the form of religious and metaphysical tools. In modern times, Marie Curie, in her Paris laboratories, experimented with the "piezo" properties of quartz crystal. Although she has not been honored for this advance, Marie and her brothers were the pioneers who gently ushered the crystal across the mystical threshold into today, and thus helped introduce this Age of Communications.

One unique property of quartz crystal is called *piezoelectricity*. Piezo, pronounced pee-AY-zo, comes from the Greek word *piezein*, which means to squeeze or press. The crystal generates electricity when pressure is applied and displays polarity due to its positive and negative forces. Also, electricity fed into quartz crystal generates stress which usually results in vibrations and precise oscillations. This is the major secret of radio and television broadcasting on a chosen and repeatable wavelength of energy.

For future technologies, scientists are creating not only second- and third-generation grown crystals for specific uses but also new piezo-plastics and ceramics of tremendous value. The technology seems limitless, as it well may be. The silicon chips are mentioned because they were born from the knowledge gained through earlier experiments with quartz. Still, the silicon chip may well be the key to future, practical solar-powered generators as well as yet undreamed-of uses.

The mineral symbol of the Communications Age is quartz crystal, an ancient, secret metaphysical tool now in full bloom as the basic foundation of electronic technology. In previous times, the wizards and medicine men depended upon quartz crystals to catalyze their miracles. Our modern scientific community also seems to regard the crystal with this same reverence.

Texas Instrument, a giant electronics firm, displays a sign in their laboratories which reads "We do not believe in miracles, we rely on them." Texas Instruments is a leading supplier of silicon integrated circuits, called "chips." Fortunately, an abundance of raw silicon is available for this purpose. The chips are manufactured from thin slices of specially prepared silicon ingots.

Pure ingots are made by dipping a seed crystal into molten liquid silicon maintained at a temperature of 2,600 degrees Fahrenheit in a crucible. The silicon melt crystallizes at that contact point with the seed crystal, which is constantly rotated as it is slowly pulled upward out of the crucible. The attached crystallized silicon emerges as a glowing, round, fat ingot pulled from the pot at a slow speed of a few inches per hour.

Electronic industries use enormous amounts of both "pulled" silicon ingots and grown quartz crystals. During World War II, the United States alone used more than 50 million quartz crystals for communications in military applications. Today, the electronic quartz crystals are grown worldwide in laboratories to meet the demand. These laboratories supply a near perfect, controlled environment for crystal growth, and Mother Nature does the rest.

THE SONG

Breathless, I listen
To the singing voices
Pouring forth their lilting cascade
Of praises to life.

Life that twists and turns
In myriad manners,
Sometimes faltering,
Sometimes darting in blinding speed.
Life that ever yearns for perfection
In its hungry searching.
The life of continuity,
Always ascending higher and higher
Into ecstasies of blissful illumination.

I stand in awe of this praise to creation.
I listen as I watch the stars,
The scintillating crystals of the Universe
Grandly waltzing
Across the blue black sky.

They sing and dance
In perfect rhythm
To the eternal progression
Of every soul.

—Frank Dorland, 1979

NATURAL AND REFINED QUARTZ CRYSTAL

Abundant stocks of natural quartz crystal may be refined into solid blocks of perfectly clear electronic quartz crystal, which is very scarce. The refining method is called hydrothermal transport growth. It is actually a process mimicking Mother Nature's way of growing crystals, but the scientists have added controls and safeguards to assure production of the highest class of uncontaminated electronic crystal block known.

Natural Creation of Quartz Crystals

Mother Nature creates crystals by volcanoes and earthquakes, which change the magma flow and heat and pressure within the earth's crust. When heat approaches 300 degrees centigrade, crystalline quartz masses will dissolve in the mineralized ground waters, which at that temperature would be superheated to a steam pressure of about 20,000 pounds per square inch. The dissolved quartz solution will migrate to a cooler area where it will grow upon a suitable matrix or seed crystal. If there is nothing to grow on, the dissolved mass upon cooling will "grow" on itself and develop into a crystal with a point at either end. At Herkimer, New York, these crystals are called Herkimer Diamonds.

Artificial Creation of Quartz Crystals

Since it may take thousands of years after the crystal has grown deep into the ground for it to be found, scientists now grow large refined blocks of highest quality crystal for the electronic market. The current refining process takes place in huge autoclaves.

Cleaned and crushed quartz crystal is placed on the bottom of a large steel cylinder. Mineralized water is added until the container is about 85 per cent full. Thinly sliced seed crystals are then suspended at the top of the cylinder and a pressure lid is securely attached. The steel cylinder is then lowered into an explosion-proof cell and the heat is turned on. Although it requires very high heat of 1,710 degrees centigrade to melt quartz crystal, it readily dissolves in mineralized water at only 300 degrees centigrade if the container is pressurized at 20,000 pounds per square inch.

The dissolved crystal will transport itself toward the cooler area where the undissolved crystal seeds are suspended. In only a few weeks, large blocks of highest quality electronic crystal have grown upon the seeds while leaving any contamination down at the bottom of the cylinder. By using the proper minerals and controls, this process can be used to grow colored crystals as well as the clear ones. Highest quality citrines, golden yellows, blues, greens and amethyst crystals have been recently grown in Russia, Germany, Japan, France and the United States.

Lapidarians and gemologists claim that refined quartz is synthetic. This of course is not true, for it is only quartz crystal refined to its highest quality.

Bottom of Autoclave
Shown before heavy insulation is packed around the steel shell. The vertical strips at the
bottom are electric heating strips. The steel shell sits atop a heating pad. Electrical supply
cables are visible at left. When the insulation is packed around the steel shell, none of this
is visible.   *Photo courtesy Sawyer Research Products*

Center Walkway, Autoclave Area

On either side of the fluorescent lights at top center are monorails to carry the electric block and tackle to lift the cages out of the autoclave below. The pressure gauges are visible at the very top of the autoclave. When the crystals are finished, the steel rails at the side of the walkway fold back, the flooring is lifted, the insulation removed, the top unbolted and removed and the cage holding the crystals is lifted up and out of the steel shell via the electric lifts (not shown) on the monorail above. The metal ducts going to the roof are exhaust ducts to carry away the heat generated during the growing period.

Photo courtesy Sawyer Research Products

If we say that refined quartz is synthetic, then we must also state that refined gold is synthetic.

Both gold and natural quartz crystal are abundant, but not in the desired state of purity and size. Both gold and crystal are normally found in small sizes and greatly contaminated. For thousands of years gold has been mined and refined into the desired state of purity. The first experiments in growing and refining quartz crystals were done in 1851.

Perhaps it is the newness of refining quartz that has confused the geologists and gemologists. Most of them do not seem to understand that quartz crystal cannot be refined from anything but

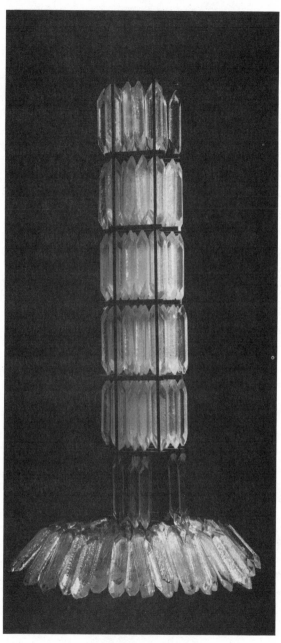

Autoclave Cage Holding Finished Crystals
The cage has been lifted out of the steel shell. The photographer has
piled loose crystals around the bottom, but this is misleading.
Photo courtesy Sawyer Research Products

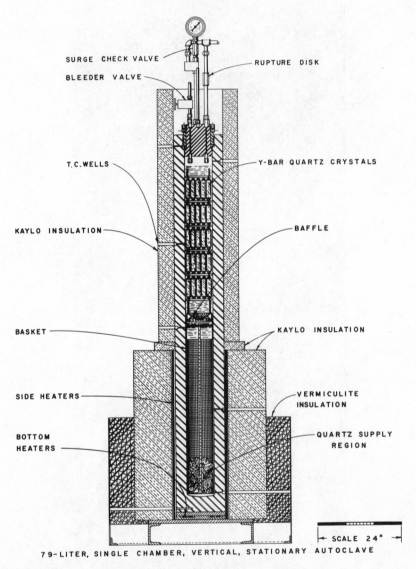

SURGE CHECK VALVE

BLEEDER VALVE

RUPTURE DISK

T.C.WELLS

Y-BAR QUARTZ CRYSTALS

KAYLO INSULATION

BAFFLE

BASKET

KAYLO INSULATION

SIDE HEATERS

VERMICULITE INSULATION

BOTTOM HEATERS

QUARTZ SUPPLY REGION

SCALE 24"

79-LITER, SINGLE CHAMBER, VERTICAL, STATIONARY AUTOCLAVE

SAWYER RESEARCH PRODUCTS, INC.

FIGURE I

Cutaway Drawing of Autoclave
Courtesy Sawyer Research Products

Workers Removing New Crystals from Autoclave
The floor and insulation have been removed to
make a "pit" around the top of the autoclave.

Photo courtesy Sawyer Research Products

quartz crystal and just like pure gold, the refining of a mineral does not change its classification to synthetic.

The scientific application of knowledge gained from experiments with crystals has resulted in a cloudburst of new products. A few examples are wristwatches and timepieces of astonishing accuracy, radio, television, telephones and the worldwide communications network, computers, word processors, sonar devices, complex medical and hospital equipment, precisely controlled aircraft and automobiles, boats and futuristic new methods of generating electrical energies.

The latest crystal news is a pill containing a temperature-sensitive device and a crystal. The swallowed pill broadcasts body temperatures continuously to a nearby receiver, which displays the constant figures for doctors and nurses.

NOTES

1. It should be noted that Edison did not actually have a black box that made things disappear. His lecture was merely stressing the variety of wavelengths of energy in existence.

2. The crystal was often carved to symbolize the first four vertebrae in the spinal columns. This was thought to be the root of great energy or power.

Crystal Applications

DIVINATION

The practice of divining is common to all ages and to all civilizations. Divination is one of the major roots of many religions and the main ingredient of others. Divination, prophecy, augury, foretelling by the casting of arrows or sticks, the throwing of dice, inspection of animal entrails, card reading, necromancy and hundreds of other practices, in and out of trance state, have been utilized.

Remember that the seed from which most religions sprang was a mystical experience of an individual such as Jesus, Buddha, or Mohammed where visions were seen and where voices were heard—visions or voices that no one saw or heard except for the chosen one. This was a divine and profound experience of unforgettable magnitude to the individual.

Egg Blowing

One fascinating form of divination little known today but once commonly practiced is known as egg blowing. This mystical performance is accomplished by puncturing a hole in each end of a raw egg. The witch doctor, shaman, or diviner—whoever is performing—takes a great breath and forcefully blows the contents of the egg out of its shell onto a cleanly swept ground. (For royalty, VIPs, etc., the smoothed ground was coated with a thin layer of crushed quartz crystal, which is a white powder when pulverized). This results in a magical pattern of splatters of raw egg which are then interpreted by the diviner to foretell the future and to give guidance. This art is, of course, similar to tea-leaf readings.

I am sure that our scientific community would ridicule this practice and the belief that the egg blobs have any intelligent meaning or message. Interestingly, some scholars have seriously suggested, after much research, that the modern scientific theory of the Big Bang is nothing more or less than a dim, genetic memory-bank event that has come to light in an inspired revelation—a vivid subconscious memory of a full-fledged egg blowing performance that is interpreted by the logical conscious mind of the scientist to explain how the whole universe began in the first place.

Dreams

One form of foretelling that has been universally accepted is divination by dreams. The Bible tells us of Solomon's dreams wherein God talked to him (for example, I Kings 3:5-15). In another chapter of the Bible, Daniel interprets Nebuchadnezzar's dreams (Daniel 2). Joseph is rightly a divining prophet when he interprets the dreams of the butler, the baker and the Pharaoh of Egypt (Genesis 41:1-37). The Bible has many such incidents—anecdotes of dream divination and prophecy and many examples of magic; but, in this holy book, magical results are called "miracles." It makes a great deal of difference whether one labels an event "magical" or "miraculous," does it not?

Divination by Crystals

One kind of divining has been generally practiced in secrecy—that involving the use of quartz crystals. Crystals have been discovered to increase intuition. Diviners and sorcerers believed that the crystals gave extra powers to the user.

Since good pieces of crystal—clear, transparent, electronic type that worked properly—were rare and hard to find, unsurprisingly, those who used quartz crystals had a common bond of secrecy among them. The priest, the royalty, the army commanders, the leaders, the witch doctors, seers and the soothsayers—those in power conspired to reserve the crystals for their own use. The best way to accomplish this was to keep the knowledge hidden as much as possible.

Inferred is an age-old conspiracy to keep crystals reserved for those privy to the secret. Printed proof of this lies in the fact that quartz crystals have never been included on any of the birthstone lists until the 20th century. Many other stones were named, but only in very recent history has quartz crystal been included.

The best crystal working tools may be carved in a great variety of shapes with the major consideration that all surfaces must be smoothed and rounded. There must not be sharp angles, sharp edges or points, because the crystal is a working piece designed to be held in the hand or worn close to or against the skin. Faceting is never used in any authentic working crystals for many reasons. Faceting is quite modern with a total history of only a few hundred years, whereas the use of rounded and smoothed metaphysical crystals dates back to prehistoric times.

When the crystal is energized, it broadcasts outward in spiral waves both clockwise and counterclockwise in all directions simultaneously. The energy is believed to flow unimpeded through curved surfaces, but flat and faceted surfaces tend to carom or ricochet the waves of energy from one flat surface to another. This ricocheting effect tends to dissipate the energy inside the crystal much like a spent pool ball. Most of the "broadcast" can't get out of the crystal!

The activation and use of crystals takes a certain amount of time and dedication as well as coordination of the mind, brain and body of the individual.

CRYSTAL BALLS

Crystal balls have played a vital role in the destiny of tribes and nations. The true knowledge about real quartz crystal tools has been orally handed down to those in the secret cliques: the brotherhoods, the priests and priestesses, the shamans, the oracles and the doctors.

The oldest known really round crystal ball was found in France in the ancient Merovingian tomb of Childeric I, King of the Salian Franks (437-481 A.D.). Childeric was an unusual ruler, as his very successful reign abounded with magical mysteries, the supernatural and legendary accomplishments. His great influence extended long after his death. As an example, at the time of the fall of the Bastille during the French Revolution, the rabble sacked the royal tombs believing they held fortunes in royal jewels. To the crowd's disgust, they found no diamonds, rubies or emeralds whatsoever, but they did discover among the royal bones small, personal crystal balls. Little did they understand the deceased royalty had placed higher value on their crystals than on adorning gemstones.

Childeric's potent influence reached down through time to Napoleon Bonaparte, who commanded that his elaborate coronation robes be studded with some tiny solid gold figures of honeybees. These identical gold bees had earlier been taken out of Childeric's tomb.

The crystal ball is not always perfectly round as usually seen in jewelry store windows and depicted in comic strips. Many real working crystals are entirely hand carved, and are not machine lapped to optical roundness. They do not need a fancy stand to stay put because their roundness is irregular and thus they do not easily roll.

The optically perfect sphere, which is very ornamental and expensive if made of real quartz electronic crystal, is quite rare. Actually over 99 per cent of the world's crystal balls are imitations made of glass, plastic, or what is called lead crystal, which is glass with a lead content. We know that lead shields and protects against rays and that glass is an excellent insulator. None of these imitation balls are even slightly capable of reacting to body and mind energies. They don't work; so, obviously, people laugh at crystal balls.

Some psychics say they do not need a crystal ball to divine; they can use a cup of water or a glass of wine. They look at the reflections on the surface of the liquid and receive their messages that way. This they believe and, for them, this is fine. (It should be noted that surface reflections mirror the five-sense physical world, not the spirit world.) I will later explain exactly what happens when a real crystal ball is properly used. However, I will first explain how the crystal became round in the first place, because, as I stated before, most authentic crystal balls are not perfectly round.

Let us go back in time and imagine a scene taking place in a castle. The royal prophet is telling the king how to run his affairs and the ruler solemnly takes his advice, causing his kingdom to flourish and prosper. Everything is running beautifully because the prophet is a very smart metaphysician and very capable psychic. He consults a mystical quartz crystal in the privacy of his chambers in the castle to solve his problems. The king eventually finds out that his royal prophet has this transparent crystal that is kept in a sack hanging by a leather cord around his neck.

The cord is rather long so the crystal hangs near the pit of his stomach. The king summons him and say that he, too, would like to have one of these shining crystals. The prophet says, "Of course, yes, your Majesty," and then he thinks for a long, long time as to what to do about this situation. If the king has a crystal, and if the king knows how to use the crystal, perhaps the prophet could be out of a job. So, the royal prophet tells the king, "Your Majesty, you are the perfect ruler, so we will carve you a crystal befitting your station in life—a perfect crystal like the mystical spheres that contain the sun and the moon and the stars and the planets."

The prophet then ordered the royal stonecutter to take a large piece of quartz crystal and carve it to perfection. The king was very pleased when he saw it and asked, "How do I work with this crystal?"

The prophet replied, "Your Royal Majesty, you must prepare yourself for at least seven days before using this crystal by rising daily with the morning sun, eating only of the sacred foods, and by abstaining from any wine, meat or women. You must cleanse and purify yourself. You must wait until after sundown on the seventh day of purification, then you put the crystal ball on this beautiful stand that I have made for you. Place it in the center of this white linen cloth. You shall light four candles, one at each of the four corners of the cloth, and then you shall sit back in your chair and gaze at the crystal. Repeat these secret syllables I shall give to you. After that, the crystal ball will show you visions and will answer your questions."

This story suggests how the first perfectly round crystal balls might have come into existence. The prophet did not want the king to know the correct way of using the crystal, so he furnished misleading directions.

With time and use, however, the natural crystals would come to have all the corners and sharp edges knocked off. They eventually became "the shapeless lump." Users found that a smoothed and polished lump of crystal transformed far greater energies than a natural crystal point with flat, faceted surfaces which ricocheted the energies internally and dissipated them rather than broadcasting the energies.

Crystal Gazing

The secrets of the crystal are many, but according to shamans and others who work with crystals, the basic, number-one secret is this—a crystal, like any electronic instrument, will never work until you turn it on. A crystal has to have energy like a radio set. The crystal gets its energy from the person using it, so you must either cup your hands around it to allow the energy from your body to activate the crystal or, better yet, pick up the crystal in your hands and hold it. Upon receiving your energy, the crystal changes its vibration from its normal pattern to a rhythm that harmonizes in sympathy with the natural vibrations of your body cells. That is one of the major secrets. A crystal ball will not work by itself sitting on a stand. A person must hold it or cup their hands around it.

Secret number two is, when you gaze at a crystal ball, rather than merely staring at it, you project your mind deeply inside it. Two different readings can be received from a crystal ball. One reading is obtained from surface reflections. The polished surface reflects whatever is in view—the people and the lights, patterns and colors. These vibrations are all on the level of the physical plane of existence which is the five-sense plane.

For a higher level reading, the crystal gazer looks deeply into the ball and mentally enters the crystal itself, concentrating only on the single purpose at hand. In this way, the five senses are subdued sufficiently to allow the psychic portions to communicate with the crystal cells. At this stage, the crystal gazer is in a deep trance state—a state of self-hypnosis wherein the crystal receives, amplifies and rebroadcasts data from the crystal gazer and other sources.

The crystal cells transmit these radio-like waves through the nervous system to the cortex cells in the gazer's brain. They are unscrambled and composed into meaningful signals which may be recognizable as pictures, words or perhaps just a sense of knowing in the conscious mind. These messages may be received from many sources but, primarily, they seem to come from the subconscious memory bank and superconscious sources. The crystal gazer himself must direct these activities and select the knowledge sought with great care.

When a question is asked and the subconscious mind is unable to answer, the crystal gazer can direct the subconscious to contact

River-Tumbled Crystal
Raw crystal often dictates shape of finished crystal.

memory banks of other individuals who may have the desired information in their files. A universal communication network is believed to exist on the subconscious level of which few are aware. This information can be obtained and reported at a future date, which means a tremendous store of information is available from this source. The rules of using the crystal are few, so psychics can develop all of their abilities in harmony with their individual personalities.

The size of the crystal is not too important, since the energy comes from the crystal operator and not from the crystal. I have carved many crystal balls of all descriptions and sizes—the optically and perfectly round newer type, and not-so-round classic style, and the hand-working crystals which are carved to comfortably fit in the palm of the hand. Any of these styles are useful tools. Most learned crystal gazers know that crystal visions are not seen with the two physical eyes, but are interpreted by the third eye—

the intuitive eye, the one that knows.

AMULETS AND TALISMANS

Major worldwide archeological expeditions have resulted in discoveries of objects generally called amulets or talismans. The use of these items is believed to have always been and remains to be universal. Their history reaches into the most remote past and touches every known race and civilization. Widespread common use of talismans is due to mankind's everlasting belief in a shadow world of spirits and magic. From the earliest times, man's conscious mind has had both a deep faith and a fear that there was far more to existence and reality than could possibly be fathomed with his limited five senses. Amulets and talismans helped man's conscious mind bridge the misty chasm separating the solid physical world from the spiritual world of gods and angels, demons and devils.

In the past, the two words "amulet" and "talisman" occasionally have been used in identical context, but today they are mistakenly interchanged. The two have a relationship but are drastically different from one another. An amulet is a charm or a lucky piece; for example, a lucky coin or rabbit's foot would properly be classified as an amulet. Amulets are worn around the neck or on bracelets and anklets as charms to give luck and ward off evil.

A talisman is much more potent than an amulet because "a talisman is an object that confers supernatural powers and protection to its user." The word supernatural is used in its common meaning, but the reader should remember that once supernatural forces are understood, they become applied natural laws. A person wearing and using a crystal talisman might be thought of as employing supernatural powers only to those not initiated into the working powers of the crystal. To the enlightened ones, the use of a crystal talisman is a perfectly normal and natural application of crystal energies in their most noble sense.

Talismans have been made out of practically every material known. Besides gemstones, there were metals, fabrics, woods, grains and hides. Common shapes were all styles of crosses, astrological symbols, including the sun and the moon, animals and fish, divinities and mystical figures. Many were engraved or lettered with magical texts. Several studies indicate the majority of these

Cross, Ankh and Other Assorted Crystal Talismans.

talismans showed supernatural powers only through the energies generated in the minds of the believers. Talismans made of electronic quartz crystal, however, are potent forces, because they have their own magnetic energy field and they do react and respond.

A quartz electronic crystal is called the "living stone" by the Chinese, probably because the crystal is in a constant state of motion (oscillation). This is inherent in a crystal through its unique latticework structure designed by Mother Nature and constructed during its growth from individual crystal cells. The scientist calls them "piezoelectronic" crystals, meaning they are capable of generating electricity through pressure. Metaphysical studies show that the crystals also react and respond to the energies broadcast from human thought waves. In other words, they behave like an ESP reflector-amplifier.

Some of the oldest known examples of talismans are pieces of flint and quartz from early Paleolithic times. These chipped and shaped pieces had a hole worked in them which would allow them to be worn suspended on a string or a leather thong. Some talismans were made as long as 500,000 years ago. Examples of carefully shaped strings of beads made of limestone and quartz were produced about 100,000 years ago.

Talisman Shapes

Talismans are carved in the form of crosses, circles, solar discs, crescent moons, triangles and pyramids, dewdrops and teardrops, hearts and other anatomical parts, fish, fowl, animals, vegetation, and so on. Out of the innumerable shapes, however, almost all are primarily based on the cross, the circle and the triangle.

The cross symbol gets its roots from the equal-armed mystic cross commonly seen as the plus sign in mathematics and the positive sign in electricity. In ancient time, the cross was the symbol of God and the mystical number four. Out of this symbol of positivity, there evolved hundreds of variations of the cross sign. In modern times, the majority of crystal talismanic crosses are carved in three basic styles—the mystic, the ankh, and the Latin cross.

Originally, the circle was a symbol of God because it has no beginning or end. Used as a solar disc or the moon sign, this also meant "God." When used as the sign of the full moon or its portion as a crescent, this symbolizes the Queen of Heaven. The triangle is the symbol of the trinity and also the pyramid and the secret sign of the builder.

Only one rigid rule exists in the proper design of crystal talismans—they must be carved with gently rounded corners without sharp edges or points. A crystal is a very personal and intimate object worn in close contact with the body. Many are worn under shirts or blouses in direct contact with the skin, and it is not unusual for small ones to be pinned to a bra or suspended between the breasts. Talismans are to be worn, and must be safe and easy to work with. A properly carved talisman should feel good in the hand and anywhere else on the body. Comfort is a basic necessity.

Colored and Colorless Talismans

The color of a talisman is important; however, it can also be meaningless. As far as electronics is concerned, color is not important because the function of a crystal talisman is to interchange the electrical energy output between itself and the various components of the human being. Normally, color neither helps nor hinders the electronic capabilities of the crystal, so, from that standpoint of energy flow, a crystal could be colored or colorless. Either would work equally well in an electronic device. However, this observation is not entirely valid when the human element is considered.

Color is very important to most individuals. This may be due partly to an accumulation of conscious tastes, likes and dislikes. A large part of it is also due to the inherited subconscious memory bank, which is rich with data from the past. As is the case with fingerprints, no two minds are identical, and it must be agreed that certain individuals have very strong feelings regarding various colors. Whenever crystal psychic tools are on display, their spellbinding fascination to the human race is very evident. Individuals who may be absolute strangers to metaphysical teachings show strong reactions to certain meaningful shapes.

Even though they may be viewing these paranormal tools for the first time consciously, many individuals display a seemingly inherent, automatic knowledge of the use of crystals and how to handle them. A reaction is obviously taking place, and a pleasant one at that. Conversely, others may display aversion, despondency or fear. In this regard, the genetic subconscious memory bank should not be trifled with and any probing experiments in that area must be carefully observed and controlled.

Talismans and the Chakra Centers

During the Piscean Age, the psychic receptor centers were located mainly in the solar plexus area. When questioned about their psychic sensitivity, many a seer indelicately explained, "It's a gut feeling; I get it right in the pit of my stomach." In this new Communications Age, the receptor center is expected to elevate itself to the heart or even higher. This means the favored location for wearing a crystal talisman would be anywhere between the solar plexus and the heart chakra. This places the suspended crystal in the best position to gain input and output to and from both areas.

The word "chakra" means "the circle of Vishnu"—a spinning dynamo-like wheel. Chakras are usually illustrated as round, spinning discs of color, but they are also symbolically shown as a lotus blossom with a varying number of petals.

The chakra centers are believed to be located on or near the vital spinal column. The spinal chord is called the "sacred rod of mysteries." Some examples of this mystical power are mentioned as "The Rod of Brahman," "Aaron's Rod," and "The Rod of Moses." Legends tell us that the 33rd Masonic degree evolved from the dim past as a gathering of the forces through the 33 vertebrae of the spinal column, culminating in a concentration of total power in the skull. The Hindus call this ascending energy the "Kundalini," the power of life and the rising serpent.

There are seven beneficial chakra centers of energy:

1. The root chakra is located at the base of the spine and is called the sacred ganglion and known as the coiled sleeping serpent, the Kundalini power. The color is fiery red; the sound is the chirping of crickets. The symbolic lotus has four petals. Its function is regenerative power, and is an earth sign.

2. The spleen chakra, or prostatic plexus, is located over the spleen. The color is yellow-orange and the sound is the buzzing of bees. The lotus has six petals. The function is the utilization of natural energies. It is a water sign.

3. The solar plexus chakra or the navel. The colors are reds and greens. The sound is a heavy drone, deeper than bees. The symbolic lotus has ten petals. The function is the emotions and control over interior cells. It is a fire sign. This has been the psychic receptor center for the Piscean Age.

4. The heart chakra or cardiac plexus. The color is golden sunlight and the sound is that of a pleasant flute. This lotus has 12 petals. This air sign's function is control over the winds. This is the eventual psychic receptor center for the Age of Aquarius or Communications Age we are now entering.

5. The throat chakra or pharyngeal plexus. The color is silvery blue and the sound is a medium-pitch bell note. This lotus has 16 petals. The function is the control over the etheric elements, and hence it is an ether sign.

6. The brow chakra or cavernous plexus. The color is golden-yellow and purple and the sound is that of a deep, temple gong. The lotus has 96 petals. The mastery of all elements is its function, and the sign is that of the mind.

7. The crown chakra is located in the center of the top of the head. It contains all the colors and so approaches pure white light.

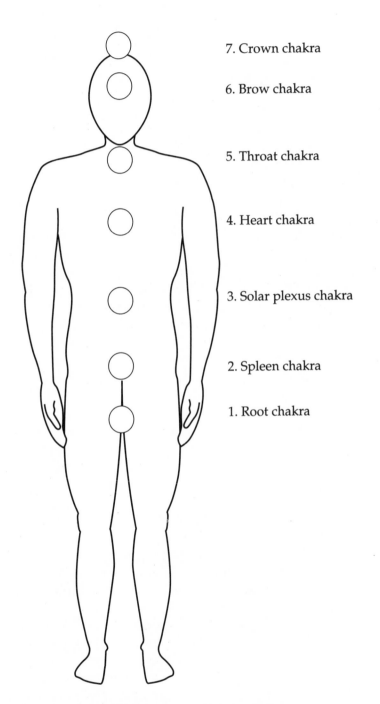

7. Crown chakra

6. Brow chakra

5. Throat chakra

4. Heart chakra

3. Solar plexus chakra

2. Spleen chakra

1. Root chakra

The Chakras and the Nervous System

The sound is the steady roar of the distant ocean. This symbolic lotus has 972 petals, thus approaching the perfect 1000. The function is the mastery of the gift of complete understanding. The sign is that of total refinement into eventual perfection.

While the chakras are thought to be specifically reactive to quartz crystals, it should be understood that crystals will receive and broadcast energies from any location on the body. This means that a crystal in close contact with the skin in any area is capable of functioning on an exchange-of-energy basis. It then follows that certain locations on the body are used mainly because of tradition, belief, taste and suitability. From a practical standpoint, the widely accepted position of the suspended crystal talisman is between the solar plexus and the heart chakra.

A viewpoint in total opposition to the chakra system exists in several secret brotherhoods. Their doctrines state that the chakras are imaginary and do not exist. They believe a long line of promoters first adapted part of an ancient belief and then glamorized and romanticized it. This created a new enticing program of instructions to enrich the curriculum of their private run-for-profit mystery schools.

Using subtle indoctrination and dominant psychological insinuations, the teachers induced a psychic state of belief that caused the students to think they experienced the opening and functioning of their respective chakras. Vivid statements describing opening petals, whirling wheels and spinning colored propeller-like vortices of power have been sworn to in great numbers. Today, the chakras are widely taught and believed by millions of people in almost all parts of the globe.

Some brotherhoods quietly state the roots of the chakra system originated in the most ancient of prehistoric times from belief that sex and the divine were heavenly intertwined forces. They thought sexual arousal would release holy energies held captive in a secret place at the base of the spine. These freed spiritual pulsations would then rise up and flood the body.

When this saturation was complete, pressure would mount until remaining powers still stored at the base of the spine would be released to shoot up the spinal column and flash throughout the crown area and the third eye. From this basic belief of energy flowing from the base of the spine upward throughout the body, a complex system of ten energy centers was developed.

In modern times, seven chakras remain in teachings. Three of the original ten were dropped when the chakra system was brought to the Western world, because they were believed to be an offensive liability.

The deleted three energy centers were crowded together at the base of the spine, where they supposedly controlled the organs of elimination and ejaculation. Their major use was reserved entirely for black magic. Excrement was mixed with urine and semen to obtain a paste ointment which was secretly smeared on or near personal possessions of the intended victim. This was supposed to insure the potency of the evil spell. As ridiculous as it may seem, this practice is still being resorted to. Occasionally while investigating a crime, the police will discover a foul ointment smeared on or near the scene. Hopefully, they would realize that black magic could be involved, as this should be a leading clue. That black magic rites of many descriptions are in everyday usage in practically every large city in the world is shocking, and the practice seems to be growing.

A third and quite recent viewpoint about the chakra system comes from some modern metaphysical practitioners who feel the chakras do exist but not as commonly represented. They think the chakras are actually electrical energy nerve network junctions. They also feel that, instead of a limited number of seven, there are over 7,000 of them in each human being. In addition, they say that many of these major nerve junctions coexist with common acupuncture or acupressure locations.

COLORS

The color vibration theory is widely practiced in many variations, and long lists of color symbolizations have been printed. These lists do not necessarily hold true for all individuals, because various colors have different meanings in different countries and civilizations. Therefore, each person should know his or her genealogical background in order to interpret a personal, built-in color belief system. As a guideline, however, there are the standardized symbolic meanings of the basic colors for reference. (As in most therapies, the colors may be custom mixed. In other words, a crystal may be wrapped in a green cloth to give independence and then both crystal and green cloth wrapped in a yellow cloth to give hopefulness and understanding.)

Gray: Protection, quiet, avoidance of conflicts, peace-making, placidity and serenity.

Black: Neutralizing, simplification, reduction to basics, and subdued emotions.

Blue: Harmony, tranquility, intimacy, spiritual satisfaction, forgiveness and peace.

Red: Vitality, strength, excitement, physical satisfaction and enthusiasm.

Green: Achievement, success, independence, resilience and control.

Yellow: Ambition, hope, understanding, warmth and affection.

Violet: Sentimental, romantic, idealistic, tender, spiritual strength and fantasy.

Brown: Safety, security, indulgence, restfulness, tranquility and conservativeness.

White: Purity.

Metaphysical white is much like daylight, which is composed of all the colors of the rainbow. Metaphysical white has all the vibrations of every color including black, so white is the complete vibration. Since the benefits of color therapy depend largely on the control of mind over matter, a white cloth can be used in place of any other color. Of course, the degree of success depends entirely on the training and abilities of each individual to be fully in control of the total mind. In this case, the total mind includes all aspects of the five-sense conscious mind and the subconscious mind with its genetic memory bank.

In most cases, the use of individually selected colors as needed is the simplest and most popular approach. For those who feel sure of their mastery of the mind, a colorless white cloth may be used for all symbolism and purposes, keeping paramount the importance of verbally programming the intent when wrapping the crystal. Many benefits of crystals are not automatic; they must be created, well-planned and controlled by the mind.

PENDULUMS, DIVINING RODS AND AURAS

Pendulums

Another use for crystals is the divining pendulum. Crystal pendulums are generally small. Tiny crystals are very reactive, while large, heavy crystals are sluggish due to their weight. Crystal pendulums have either a silver loop or a hole through the top of the crystal so a string can be threaded through the hole. The string should not be too long because the crystal pendulum must hang close enough to the aura to receive energy from the magnetic flux surrounding the body, but long enough to swing freely. Generally, three or four inches of string is more than adequate on almost any crystal pendulum, and silk or cotton is the preferred material. The crystal pendulum works because it responds to output from the mental and physical energies of the body.

At this time, an explanation about the functioning of a psychic pendulum is necessary. One object that will work is a magnetized iron carpet tack; the magnetism gives the tack a positive and negative magnetic field. Another would be a magnetized darning needle. Such a needle could float on a little pool of oil and be used as a compass because it is attracted to magnetic north by its polarity and the properties of magnetism. Any small object that can be magnetized to give it a north and south pole or a positive and negative end can be used as a pendulum.

The reason a crystal is superior to other materials is the fact that, not only does the crystal have positive and negative properties, but also every cell in the crystal repeats the pattern. The crystal is believed to respond to the energy of the pendulum operator and to vibrate in harmonic pulsations with the human body cells. As far as we know, a quartz electronic crystal on the end of a string is probably the finest pendulum that anyone could ever use due to its great responsiveness and ability to relay its contact with the subconscious memory bank through its swinging directional ability.

Before anyone ever works with a crystal pendulum, prayers and mental and spiritual cleansing is highly recommended. It is an earth-shattering experience to many people who start using the pendulum as a game and find out they actually are really getting answers to their questions. The experience completely frightens them.

If the reader would like to use the pendulum, I trust you understand what you are getting into. If you do not have a deep understanding of the metaphysical world, I suggest that you do not use the pendulum until you are more experienced. To use a pendulum, you should have a good substantial foundation of morality, integrity and responsibility. Additionally, background in religious beliefs, an understanding of religions, a study of magical practices, and knowledge of metaphysics in general would be helpful.

When you are using a pendulum, you are not talking only to yourself and your five senses, but you are also talking to 36 psychic senses and probing into the files of your own subconscious memory bank. You are also able to talk indirectly to your superconscious and to your metaconscious. You should be extremely careful of what you ask, because if you pursue the subject, you will probably get the answer.

Now to get back to how the pendulum is used. A crystal is suspended by a thread. You should hold the thread with your fingers, leaving about two to three inches between the top of the pendulum and the tips of your fingers. You should also have a target card—a pendulum card—as shown on the opposite page. It is round like a bull's-eye target. It has the alphabet around the outside and numbers around a smaller circle inside. The suspended pendulum swings back and forth over the card, answering questions by swinging to letters of the alphabet and thus spelling out words. It will point to numbers, specifying days, dates and digital information.

To begin, lay the pendulum card on a sturdy table so your arm will be steady. As you hold the pendulum over the center of the card, a preparatory, cleansing prayer is said. At the prayer's conclusion, a request is made that the information received will be used for a beneficial purpose and will not bring harm to anyone.

There is a real and practical reason for this. There is a law of checks and balances in the universe that keeps everything in order. This law seems to automatically tally credits and debits. When entering into the metaphysical vibrations, this law becomes a dominant force—an unrelenting force that commands respect.

You speak out loud to the crystal pendulum and ask, "Would you like to work with me today?"

The pendulum will answer either "Yes" or "No." With a yes answer, it will swing forward and backward as one would nod the head for "Yes." For "No," it will swing sideways, back and forth, as if shaking the head "No." There are some individuals with a genetic background who could reverse these signals, so each one

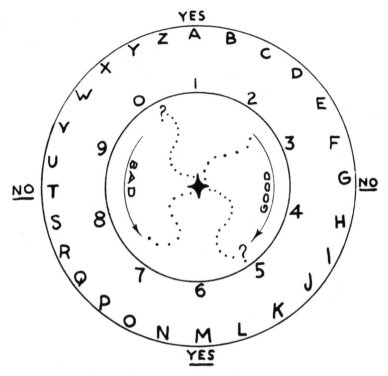

Card for Use with Pendulum

should experiment to determine their own interpretation of the crystal's signals.

The question is asked out loud, because it is better to audibly talk to the crystal than to silently think. As you ask the question, the pendulum will swing, pointing out the different letters of the alphabet for words or the numbers between 1 and 9 (plus 0) for dates and digital information.

As it swings, talking to the pendulum is constantly necessary in order to keep up the vibrations and energy flow. Thank it for each answer, because you are talking directly to the subconscious memory bank, which is not a philosopher. It doesn't think, but rather reacts. As a general rule, the subconscious reacts very nicely to good manners. So for every answer it gives, say "Thank you. Now would you tell me the rest?" "Please proceed," "Thank you very much." In this manner the pendulum practitioner keeps the energy flowing smoothly.

With diligence and time it is beneficial and possible to determine the name of the individual's subconscious or, rather, the name the subconscious would like to be called. This helps the individual and the subconscious to work together more easily. In this way, the individual will be rewarded with a tremendous amount of enlightenment, which will encourage him to pursue the pathway into higher and greater knowledge.

One word of caution when working with the pendulum—just because you get an answer from the subconscious does not necessarily mean that the answer is truthful. Many times, a subconscious entity will be pre-programmed to lie and deceive. To play the part of a detective and arrive at very good terms with the subconscious is necessary. After receiving the answers, ask the subconscious, "Are you telling me the truth?" and, "Thank you." "Thank you for letting me know."

It is very necessary to have a pleasant, intimate relationship with your subconscious. You are living in the same body. It is impossible to escape each other's actions, so the friendlier one can be with the subconscious and the more one can gain control, the faster one can become aware of his existence and purpose and realize how to achieve fulfillment in this life, know truth, and experience happiness and perfect satisfaction.

When you first use a pendulum, write down the letters and numbers which the pendulum swings toward. Since the swing will always point to two numbers or two letters—one at each end of the swing—it is common practice to write two lines of messages. With experience, the operator will sense which one of the pendulum swings is the correct one. When that time comes, only one line of written records will need to be used.

Don't be too hasty in discarding a line of letters or numbers just because they may appear to be unintelligible. I have discovered that the subconscious may answer in many languages. This has resulted in my adding foreign dictionaries to my reference library to aid in translations. I have received messages in Russian, French, Spanish, Italian, Greek, Latin, as well as in English. In my experience, Latin seems to be a preferred communication.

Dreams

Another use of the crystals is in the practice of controlling and remembering dreams. This can be accomplished by the use of many and varied "dream crystals." One common practice is simply to put a crystal underneath the pillow and sleep on it. This works, but not so well as intentionally having a crystal close to the body. As an example, a dream crystal may be attached in some manner to the left wrist. The left wrist is used because the left hand is the receiving hand in the metaphysical world. This reception has nothing to do with being right- or left-handed, but rather the left-hand side is the "receiving" side and the right-hand side is the "strength and giving" side.

In ages past, the wizard or seer would invariably sit facing the south when entering into a trance state because this would put his back to the north. His left hand, the receiving hand, would then be toward the east. At that time, it was believed that all spiritual knowledge flowed from the east. The right hand faced toward the west to ward off any danger, because the west was the direction from which all opposition and danger came. To follow tradition, the dream crystals would be attached to the left wrist, the receiving side. This is sometimes accomplished by using a little sack tied around the wrist, or by sometimes using a single crystal with a hole in it to accommodate a soft tie-string. There are many ways of attaching the crystal.

Crystals have been attached to many places on the body. Some have made a loose fitting helmet of chamois skin to wear on their head with crystals sewn into little pockets over the crown, temples, the front of the head where the third eye would be, and on the back of the head. Usually, this helmet would be only for particular study purposes or experimentation. Crystals have also been sewn into pajamas and soft belts as well.

Before dropping off to sleep each night, the dream crystals should be programmed to affect your body cells. It is believed that the crystals repeat their instructions continuously through the night, thus stimulating and influencing the dream state to function as directed. It is also important to program the crystal to direct the mind to bring the memories back across the dream threshold and into consciousness upon awakening. Since the crystals are being worn around the left wrist, you would program them by placing the fingers of your right hand on the crystals and talking to them out loud. Tell them what you want in your dreams and also what you do not want.

If you want to dispel any nightmares or bad dreams of any kind that recur, forcefully direct your desires to eliminate these unwanted dreams and demand they be permanently discarded. Persist and beneficial dreams will take their place. The creative fields respond beautifully to dream crystals, and this method is recommended for any artistic pursuit. As you sleep, you can be gently exposed to influences and inspirations in any chosen art or science. Those who have benefited most say it is necessary to capture the dream inspirations of the night because they vanish on awakening. Use a tape recorder or pencil and note pad to record the dreams while still half asleep.

Divining Rods

Crystal divining rods are basically similar to any divining rod—a stick, a copper rod, or a slender bronze bar. The crystal is added to the very tip of the divining rod which increases its sensitivity and usefulness. These rods can be used to divine the surfaces of the earth to disclose hidden deposits of water, oil, gas or minerals. They can also be used to check out the extent of an individual's aura.

The most common type of rod is simply a pair of brass rods with a pistol-like grip to be held loosely in the hands. At the tips are a matched pair of quartz crystals. The magnetism of the body will pass downward through the metal rods while being held in the hands. When this energy reaches the crystal tip, the crystal will vibrate on a frequency compatible with the body that originated the energy. However, the amount of bronze or copper between the hands and the crystals induces what is called "a damping effect" which aids greatly in the detection of outside energies.

The exterior energies may come from almost any source, such as gold, silver, copper, water or oil—indeed, anything that the individual is specifically looking for, even lost objects. The instructions for using divining rods are quite well known. The purpose of this book is not to explain the use of divining rods. We will leave others to that, but we will say that, when there is a crystal on the end of the rod, the crystal simply amplifies and increases the magnitude of the response and makes the rod a more valuable tool.

Measuring Auras

When using the divining rod to measure the physical aura of a human being, the individual being measured should stand in front of the operator or sit in a chair. The tips of two divining rods are slowly brought toward the left- and the right-hand side of the individual at shoulder height. When they approach the subject's body, the crystals enter the edge of the auric field, which feeds a new and different energy to the crystals. This causes the crystals to change vibrations slightly and slightly "kick back." This can be sensed by the operator. This change tells the operator when the crystal tips touch the edge of the aura.

The operator should slowly move the crystal tips upward over the shoulders, along the neck and up over the head, where the two crystal tips will automatically cross. With care, the operator can keep the crystal tips at the boundary where the change of vibrations is most apparent. In this way, the outline of the human aura can be traced in the air, usually two to six inches deep.

By measuring the aura several times and by talking at the same time on different subject matters, it is easily shown that the human aura constantly changes size and energy depending on likes and dislikes, love, fear and hate. The aura also changes colors as well as size and intensity. Of course, this magnetic flux which surrounds the body has some definite relationships to the health, well-being and balance of the individual. Therefore, measuring and studying the aura of a person is much more than a parlor game.

Most of the people I have met believe that auras exist, although most cannot see them. Possibly some people see the aura but ignore it in their conscious mind. Animals apparently see the auras of people and other animals as part of their warning system. If a dog can see auras, I feel that any human can do the same. Since the aura wraps around the body like a cocoon, no hard edges exist.

Most people focus their eyes on clearly defined sharp outlines. If a person would carefully look at any living thing—animals, humans, trees or shrubs—they will see its aura. Even a transformer attached near the top of a telephone pole has a visible flux field, much like an aura, because of its flowing electricity. The aura usually looks hazy and mirage-like, with layers of color, appearing pale but very rich in saturation.

Here is a tip that might be of help if you want to look at auras. Never focus your eyes on the subject. Always look just past the edge, and either focus your eyes at a distance or do not focus them. When looking for the aura of a person, look closely near the head or near the shoulders, but keep your concentration six to eight inches away from them and look into space with your eyes unfocused. With a little effort, anyone will soon find out that all living things have more than one outline.

CRYSTALS IN HEALING

Miracles and Placebos

The placebo effect, a psychological reaction to treatment that results in improved conditions of the patient, is one of the most thoroughly documented phenomena in medical history. Purveyors of a wide variety of placebos have always existed. Early druggists concocted sugar pills in a wide variety of sizes, shapes and colors for treatment of various complaints. Amazing testimonials have been written about the success of these fabulous pills, disclosing what may have been the most harmless medicine available. Still, in the late 19th and early 20th century, commonly practiced medical treatments were dangerous, harmful and sometimes fatal. Enormous improvements and radical advances have occurred since those days for which both the doctors and their patients are grateful.

In modern medicine the placebo effect still remains as one of the top factors in the successful treatment of patients. Smart doctors know the importance of the patient's full confidence in the physician. Equally important is the physician's confidence in the treatment being administered. In addition, the physician must have enough charisma to communicate this understanding to the patient and staff. Confidence, communication and faith are the secret keys to the awesome powers of a great physician. When belief psychology is strong, the entire communications system of the patient is stimulated, including the cellular level as well as the subconscious and the conscious mind. In critical survival cases called miraculous, an induced will to live has been observed and experienced.

Gemstones have been used in the healing arts for many ages. Research indicates whatever value received from such a treatment should be classified as the placebo effect. This power has been the faithful servant of medicine men, witch doctors, shamans and faith healers for ages. There is one outstanding exception in gemstone healing and that is the live, electronic working crystal which actually responds to energies sent out from the body cells and the mind. No other gemstone does.

While the placebo effect is strong proof of the powers of the mind over matter, the use of a live, working crystal in the healing arts is doubly awesome indeed. When both the patient and the healer order well-being and health for the body through the crystal, the crystal responds to its orders by amplifying and broadcasting a continuous stream of commands to the electronic communications network of the physical body. This constant flow of commands to re-energize the immune system and rebalance the body chemistry can work miracles of recovery.

Of course, this is best used in addition to and in harmony with modern medical diagnosis and treatment by a licensed physician of choice. The crystal does not replace any medical treatment, yet remains a valuable tool to bolster and reinforce messages to the mind and soul as well as the body and all the remaining sensitive elements that contribute to the well-being of the individual. For the most part, modern medicine does not either recognize the significance of crystals nor attempt to treat with crystals. But there are a few promising breakthroughs!

Quartz Crystals

The term "medicine man" is a catchall title which includes witch doctors, magicians, priests and shamans. A medicine man plans, controls and produces the religious affairs of his followers, for he acts as their communication pipeline to the supernatural. He or she, as the case may be, is also a soothsayer, diviner and healer of mental and physical ills. Another important part of the practice is the protection from the hostile energies of sorcery and black magic.

Sometimes those classified as priests ignore their healing responsibilities and specialize only in the spiritual mediation between humans and the divine. Witch doctors, magicians and shamans do not normally do so, as a large portion of their practice includes the healing arts.

A good medicine man is a combination of medical doctor, psychologist and showman. There is no question about the effectiveness of a full-fledged performance of a costumed medicine man accompanied by fire, smoke and drums. The final results are also impressive; the production is tailored to the believed needs of the consumer and is often fruitful.

One classical tool of his trade is quartz crystal, and examples may be found in many natural history museums. A hand-held crystal is a favorite device. This crystal could be almost any shape or color, but the clear, electronic, transparent crystal is more powerful than the translucent kind, which may have no power at all except what is imagined. One popular form is a crystal with one smoothly rounded end while another tapers down to a semi-sharp point, somewhat resembling a child's toy wooden top. In fact, an Indian artifact exhibit in the United States displays one of these healing crystals labeled as an Indian child's top, for some strange reason! The purpose of the rounded end is to project healing energies over a broad, radiating area while the opposite pointed end would allow concentration of energies in a small condensed spot.

The Fairy Godmother's wand in Walt Disney's productions could easily have been inspired from a shaman's magical crystal wand as used by many tribes of American Indians. These wands are long, slender rods of bone or wood tipped with a small quartz crystal point. The crystal tipped wands were used in many religious ceremonies, including healing of the sick. They were also called into very serious service four times a year when they were ceremoniously waved at the heavens to change the seasons.

Anything powerful enough to change winter into springtime would naturally conquer most illness in short order. This is not a facetious statement. Any mighty symbol that impresses the subconscious mind can be used to direct it to rebalance the body chemistry, thus aiding in restoring depleted energies and helping to conquer illness. More than psychosomatic healing, the subconscious commander is capable of ordering natural immunity reserves of the body cells to increase and act whenever needed. This sophisticated application of a natural law can be triggered by a medicine man, doctor or psychologist with several doctorates. The end result is the same—potent medicine.

Almost any good crystal used as a talisman or for meditation can be pressed into service as a healing crystal. Since the crystal is a tool that responds to mental energies, the direction and control of the healer triggers the crystal into working as a healing generator. Some healers prefer a special, individual crystal for their sessions and many like to have another small, hand-held crystal reserved for diagnosis. The diagnostic crystal is preferably held in the left

Crystal-Tipped Magic Wand
Thought to be Chumash Indian, from Santa Barbara Museum

hand (the receiving hand) and slowly passed over the body of the patient without touching, held about two inches from the skin. With practice, a healer can sense the unbalanced areas of the body through the amplified crystal response.

Many times the crystal will indicate problems in an area where the patient has no complaint. This usually means that the crystal has located the area where the trouble originates even though the physical pain may be somewhere else. Crystal diagnosis essentially relies upon pulsed signals broadcast from the spiritual body mixed with vibrations from the magnetic flux field surrounding the body cells. Essentially, crystal diagnosis is a report on the immediate condition of the spiritual body. The physical body copies its spiritual twin; thus, a crystal diagnosis quite often indicates problems of the physical body as well.

Crystals especially designed and carved for healing may have both concave and convex curves. They always have smoothly rounded surfaces with a noted lack of sharp edges or points. The gently rounded broad area broadcasts the healing rays in a wide pattern. A semi-pointed area is often carved to allow a concentrated beam of healing energies to be touched on a small spot.

To send healing energies, hold the crystal in the right hand because this is generally the sending hand. With practice, a healer can send energies through either the left or the right hand. Some excellent healers use two crystals, one in each hand. This requires deliberate control over the subconscious mind, which, from traditional habit, is believed to automatically direct outgoing energies to the right hand.

Small, individual crystals are used to program specific aid for individual health or mental problems. The small crystals are then kept close to the body by being worn, carried in the pocket, or pinned to a garment. Many small crystals have been especially carved to be pinned to a brassiere or other undergarment. This insures that the crystals are always there, close enough to the body to function as intended.

Many healing practitioners believe a ceremonial treatment adds potency if confined to a protected space. To achieve this goal, a magic ring was devised, a "crystal ring." This ring is actually a very soft rope about 24 feet long with polished crystals attached to the rope at about 18-inch intervals or closer. The patient sits upright in a chair and the crystal rope is laid on the floor delineating a ring around the person. If the patient is confined to bed, the crystal rope is laid on the floor surrounding the bed.

The healing service is then conducted, the length and type of ceremony depending upon the healer and patient. Some services can be very elaborate and include lighted candles, sprinkled holy water, musical interludes, prayers and chants. The magic ring or circle remains in use today very much as it was in ancient times. Stonehenge, Indian medicine wheels, the wedding ring, and the zero are but four examples.

The circle or zero may be the most astounding concept ever emerged from man's mind. And, what is the zero but a circle containing nothing—and nothingness was the chaos from which creation emerged. The zero or circle denotes the absence of anything and, having nothing, emerges in a combination of digits from one to nine to create orderliness out of confusion.

Electronic Quartz Crystal Healing/Working Tools
For healing and acupressure

The digit and the simple zero are the two teamed elements that have made complex mathematics and the computer possible. This includes all the rest of the digital-based developments of modern electronic wizardry. The zero is a supreme magical symbol that unquestionably works. By creating a circle with the crystal-studded rope, a metaphysical area is created in which everything inside is complete and whole. All desirable energies can be contained and protected within the sphere, while all undesirable energies can be banished and locked outside. This creates an ideal environment in which the spiritual healer can readily perform.

The ends of the crystal rope must touch or lie across each other to fully close the circle. Some healers like to tie a ceremonial knot to insure the circle staying closed throughout the entire healing service and without being accidentally kicked open by a clumsy accident. Whatever takes place during this treatment is designed for the healing of the spiritual body of the person.

Of course, to balance and heal the spiritual body becomes a very difficult task when the physical body is suffering from pain, hunger and disease. The five senses pour out messages of discomfort to the brain, filling it with torment and leaving little room for spiritual thoughts. This condition is balanced by the equal problem of healing the physical body when the spiritual twin is sick and abused. The zenith of healing may be reached when the two bodies are simultaneously treated in planned coordination.

Crystals have found their way into modern therapy through the hands of excellent psychologists and healers. The once wide gap between standard medical doctors and the spiritual healers has narrowed considerably. When the gap is finally closed, the public will benefit greatly as will the medical doctors, psychologists and spiritual healers. When illness strikes, the complete person needs to be healed. All of us are a composite of physical, mental and spiritual energies. To be totally well requires the attention to the total being. We cannot treat an illness piecemeal and delude ourselves that we did a good job. The truth is finally becoming more and more obvious to everyone.

Animal Healing

Crystals have been used in the healing of animals. In one case, a small dog suffering from arthritis could barely manage to crawl out of his bed for meals. His owner had previously used crystals in healing humans and reasoned that her pet dog might also respond. She knitted a tiny bag and placed a crystal in it. The bag was designed to be attached to the dog's collar. She then patiently held her pet in her lap and talked to it about getting well and feeling no more pain. She held the dog's paw in contact with the crystal in her hand as she talked, thereby programming both the crystal and the dog. She reported that three days later the dog could romp and play both upstairs and downstairs in a rather sedate way.

I have firsthand information about this incident and wish to state that, although an unusual incident, the healing of pets or other animals in this fashion is possible.

Certain requirements of faith and tender care are involved. First, this particular lady is a very understanding psychic practitioner as well as a fine healer. The pet dog is closely attuned to her. For the crystal to be effective, the pet would have to understand, to a degree, and feel the warmth, love and purpose of the programmed talk given by his mistress. The association of the human mind with the animal mind coupled with the crystal amplification carried the message of healing to the cells of the pet. At all times, the healer must be dominant as well as confident and in full control.

MEDITATION AND THE CRYSTAL

In its historical sense, meditation has been practiced mainly by ascetics, mystics, hermits and saints. Generally, meditation was considered as much too dangerous for common people. Meditation was officially discouraged for the Christian layman, although encouraged for members of certain religious orders and saints such as St. Ignatius or St. Theresa. St. John described meditation as leading to "the dark night of the soul." Other vivid labels were "the mystic death" and "the descent into Hell."

Teachers of meditation as well as spiritual leaders generally agree that dangers really do exist in meditative practices, especially for those who lack firm foundation and stability. A healthy individual with some background of basic religious training has a chance to find meditation rewarding. The chances are increased if a well-balanced concept of morality and integrity is supported by a little philosophy.

I believe that properly taught and practiced meditation will certainly enrich the spiritual and physical life of any normal healthy person if given a fair chance. Meditation will induce an altered state of consciousness, and like hypnosis, drugs or anything else with power, meditation can be improperly and erratically taught and used. At this point, meditation can become dangerous. The purpose of this book is not to teach meditation, but rather to shed a little light on the uses of crystal to amplify the benefits of meditation.

Originally, meditation was taught orally. Finally, about 1,900 years ago, the oral recitations were formalized and assembled into written instructions. Under the classic definition only two types of meditation exist; one is productive and the other is nonproductive. This still remains true today. Although meditation teachings have digressed into hundreds of various styles, they all remain either productive or nonproductive.

For those who may be temporarily mentally or physically exhausted, the nonproductive meditation is a great recuperator. Experts state that 15 minutes of nonproductive meditation can give the benefits of two or more hours of rest. The productive meditation is at its greatest glory when used to solve creative endeavors in the fields of music, fine arts, fine literature, scientific achievements, philosophy and theosophy.

We have been asked many times as to who could benefit the most from meditation. The answer is, anyone who really wants to accomplish something; even the reaching of one tiny goal can be helped through meditation. There are always ways to improve every pursuit and practice. Endless numbers of wonderful advances have not even been thought of as yet. The understanding of philosophy, existence and God are still muddied with unclear answers. For most, meditation is an exercise of the free mind, a lighted path to a better tomorrow. The use of crystal in meditation reflects and amplifies the light and clarity of the revelations.

A simple, seven-step method of meditation is given here as a classic example. The first step is to get into a position that will remain comfortable; meditations should run from 15 to 30 minutes or so. A straight-backed chair is good. In fact, almost any position is acceptable as long as you do not drift off to sleep.

After assuming the chosen position, close your eyes and say preparatory cleansing prayers. You can then enter step two, the quiet period where the five senses are conditioned and ordered to be aware of everything. Make sure that nothing will startle you out of your altered state.

When you feel that your five senses are subdued, enter step three—consisting of contemplation and quieting of the emotions. You must dispel all hatred, fear and negative force of any kind so that meditation on these destructive energies can be avoided. The emotional content of the mind must be emptied.

In step four, slow your breathing pattern to a regular, rhythmic, easy rate. Some achieve this by slowly silently repeating the words "Deep peace" on each inhalation and each exhalation: Deep—inhale. Peace—exhale. When a slow, steady breathing rhythm is obtained, the meditation can go forward into the purely mental part.

In step five, review all your thoughts at this time; then discard the thoughts on the list one by one until the most important one remains for the subject of the meditation.

Step six is the concentration period. If the meditation is to be a nonproductive one, concentrate upon the last important thought for a few moments and then totally discard it. Allow your mind to go empty. With practice, a pure zero state can be reached where there is nothing—the mind is blank. When there is no, absolutely no, mental activity, a greatly accelerated resting period of complete relaxation is produced. This is richly rewarding in times of stress.

If the meditation is to be productive, concentrate upon the final chosen thought. Study this one thought for a period of time and then allow your mind to drift off to any related matter in a completely relaxed way. Of utmost importance is that none of the above steps be made into a task. Most meditation failures come from trying too hard. Meditation must be relaxing and practically effortless to gain the finest results.

After a suitable length of time lapse, the mind is allowed to drift back to normal consciousness. Those with religious learnings always close their meditation with a prayer of thankfulness. Commonly, many meditators think they never experienced any pictures, voices or happenings and had only a blank meditation. This is almost always untrue. The voices, visions and thoughts received came in on a different plane from their normal consciousness; the experiences seem to evaporate into nothingness in the few seconds taken for the mind to cross back over the threshold.

Some teachers condition their students to use an imaginary blackboard or note pad for listing all happenings during their meditation. By mentally writing the observed events on the blackboard or note pad during meditation, the ability to bring the memories back to normal consciousness is increased tremendously because a different part of the brain was used.

Use of Quartz Crystals in Meditation

Quartz crystals are used in many ways in meditation, but the two most practical methods are to wear a crystal suspended around the neck to hang over the solar plexus and heart chakra areas, or to simply hold one in the hand. A hand-held meditation crystal should be small enough to fit comfortably in the palm of the hand. A large crystal becomes too heavy, and there is always danger of it falling to the floor.

Traditionally, the crystal is always held in the left hand, the receiving hand; however, some prefer the practice called "closing the loop." The crystal is held on the lap with the fingers of the left and the right hands touching the crystal, thus allowing the energy to flow easily from the right, outgoing hand through the crystal and into the left, receiving hand. Crystal-amplified vibrations are then routed through the body cells and mind. These same vibrations travel down the right arm to the hand where they again enter the crystal to be reflected, reamplified, and passed on into the left receiving hand again to continue to form another loop.

Some meditators sew crystals in special garments that are worn during meditation and others sew crystals inside a hat or a cap. A meditation band is a wide ribbon laid on top of the head covering it from the brow to the back. Crystals are sewn or glued to the ribbon so that they are placed over the brow and the crown chakra. Additional crystals are placed at the back of the head to reflect the energy from the brow chakra in front.

In meditation, remember that the crystal is merely a tool. The crystal is not magical in any way, even if the results seem so. The crystal does not energize anything on its own. All the energy comes from the person activating the crystal with the crystal merely reflecting and amplifying what it receives. If the crystal receives poor input, it magnifies the poverty. If it receives rich, positive input, that is what is reflected and amplified. In that case, the message finally received into consciousness is apt to be thought nothing less than fantastic.

THE MEDITATION

Go into the quiet,
Leave the world behind.
Ascend into
The limitless beyond
Where peace abides.
The shining crystal
Illuminates your way
To this secret place
Of quiet joy
And understanding.
This reflection cannot be
Measured or compared
For it is nothing.

Meditation Crystals

And yet it is
Everything.

The unfathomable mysteries
Comfort and protect,
Refresh and heal
All who enter here
Seeking truth and love.

Yes, go into the quiet
And leave the world behind.
You shall emerge again
Freshly renewed,
Knowing, gentle and strong.
                    —Frank Dorland, 1982

SAMPLE MEDITATIONS

Meditation I—Thessaly

Mabel had just lit a votive candle and turned off the lights. We were both comfortably seated in our favorite meditation chairs. I had placed an extra pillow at my back for support. The candle glowed warmly in the darkened room as together we repeated the ritual cleansing prayer which always preceded meditation. When we entered into the silence, I mentally invoked my inner source to reveal some hidden truths about the crystal skull or, indeed, anything at all about crystals.

Time slowly ticked away as I quietly observed some passing shadowy forms and stray clouds of bluish light that drifted into my awareness. At long length, I thought I had about finished a more or less fruitless meditation and should be soon returning to my conscious state.

At that time, I suddenly realized that I was no longer sitting in my chair. I was far away, elsewhere, and effortlessly floating in space. It started getting lighter and I looked around to see where I was. I looked and looked and finally discovered there was a vast stretch of water below me and in the distance there was land. I thought if I could get to the shoreline I would be far safer, so I looked around to determine how I could move from my skyborne position.

I discovered that I could see no part of me. I did not seem to have any hands, arms, legs, or torso. I must be a floating consciousness, I thought, just a big eye, an observer in the sky. If that is so I wish to observe the land, I reasoned, and almost immediately I traveled nearer to the shore. Soon I could see the beaches, a harbor, and a city by the side of the sea. It was a beautiful city with wide boulevards and gently winding, tree-lined streets. There were many trees and shrubs, and all of them seemed to be in full blossom.

I went down into the city and marveled at the profusion of multicolored blooms that covered the branches. They sparkled like jewels in the late afternoon sun, and the city seemed to be filled with joy, although I saw no one in the stores and the streets were deserted. As the twilight shadows gathered, the petals began to fall. After a little while, the ground was thickly covered with fallen petals that glistened in the waning light. I looked closely at them and was startled to discover that each petal was in reality a shining crystal. The sidewalks and the streets were covered with fallen crystals, and the branches above were now bare.

As I watched, a lone man appeared down by the harbor. He uncovered a large, wooden drum that had a wheel with sturdy spokes at one end. The man slowly pulled on the spokes which turned the drum. I soon saw that an enormous net was attached to the drum. The net had covered the whole city but was invisible as it lay on the ground. The crystals were caught in the net, like fish. After some time, the net was completely wound around the drum and the man had a great pile of crystals lying before him. A full moon brightly illuminated the scene as three women walked up from the boat in the harbor. They filled many sacks with the crystals and carried them to the boat where they were carefully stowed below. Although it was the dead of night, the three cast off and headed out to sea. As the boat sailed away, I could plainly read the name on the stern. It was in bold, white letters that spelled *Thessaly*.

Back in the city the man had unwound his net from the drum and had stretched it out over the city again. In a short while, daybreak arrived and as the sun arose in the sky it flooded the city with cheerfulness. I could see that new buds were swelling on the branches. By midday they would be blossoms, and by dusk they would be full blown. As I rose into the air to leave this city, in the distance I saw the boat called *Thessaly* sailing back into the harbor again.

* * *

Follow-up studies were made to shed some light on the implications of the above meditation. They disclosed that during the early age of mankind, Thessaly was a center for sorcery and wonderworking. Thriving mystery schools reputedly taught the secrets of the use of quartz crystals and the ability to harness the powers of the moon. This prehistoric Thessaly was a former part of the present Greece. It no longer exists, because it sank beneath the sea during a geological upheaval. European writers have possibly confused the destruction of Thessaly with the earlier cataclysm of Atlantis which sank thousands of years ago. This is thought to be long before Thessaly's sinking.

Prehistoric Thessaly should not be confused with classical Thessaly of ancient times which was the center of the Hellenic world and the home of the legends of Achilles, the Argonauts, and the Minoans. Famous landmarks included the sanctuary of Achilles, the temple of Zeus, Mount Olympus, the Oracle of Delphi, and the temple of Asclepius—the miraculous healing temple of sleep. The two Thessalys were entirely different.

Meditation 2—The Original Gods

All is darkness. All is chaos. There is nothing and yet there is everything. It is too vast and too dark to realize any form or substance. Strange bits of energized matter shoot by at astounding speeds in all directions. There seems to be no order, yet underneath it all there is a realization of a rhythm, a slow, steady pulsebeat of creation in this immense void.

Somewhere, far away, there is a tiny point of light that flickers and increases in intensity. The light grows larger and larger until it becomes a blazing orb called the sun. The light and the warmth are a beacon of hope in the long night. The mists slowly rise and reveal a spinning green planet, earth, pursuing its pathway around the sun. The green earth spins closer and closer revealing oceans of water and mountains of land.

It is a good earth, pleasing to see. Everywhere there are hills and valleys, shrubs and trees, meadows and lakes sparkling and warm in the clean light of day. It is a land of laughing waters and golden valleys. There are villages built at the edge of the lakes, teaming with men, women, and children. Each village has a temple honoring the Goddess of the Waters, who is called the Great Mother, water being the vital liquid for all life and the Mother (the female) being the essential magical one who constantly replenishes everything from nothing.

The temples are small and large. Some are built of wood and some are carved from marble and alabaster. Above all, there is one great temple. It is built on the shores of the biggest lake. It is the Mother Temple where the sacred image of the Water Goddess is worshiped.

This image is a beautiful, noble, fleshless head that glistens in the light of the temple fire. It is carved from a single piece of solid crystal. Her features are magnificent in their splendor. She is fleshless because she is all races of womankind refined into one perfect ideal. Flesh and skin relate to racial identities, not spiritual essences. The skull is the abode of the spirit, the home of the soul.

The Water Goddess is the supreme symbol of feminine power.

In every temple the sacred fire continuously burns, tended by the priestesses. It is an honor to serve at the temple, and each priestess is clothed by the villagers in fine robes that reach the ground.

The sacred fire must burn continuously to give perpetual light to the Holy Water that fills the basin that never runs dry. The alabaster basin sits on a stone pedestal directly in front of the fire. The basin is kept full to the brim by the priestesses, who constantly replenish it with lake water. All water is sacred to these people, but the water in the basin turns to magic water.

This transformation is due to a crystal immersed in the basin. The crystal also gathers the powers of the sun and kindles the sacred fires for the temples. What a potent force this is that controls both fire and water. It is an everlasting symbol of the Goddess of the Waters, the Great Mother. She is God. God is She. The eternal feminine is magnificence itself. None other than She can breathe life into the newborn of the people and the plants, the animals and the fish, and the fruits and the grains. If She were to withhold her mysterious powers, the whole world would grow old and die. She is love, She is tenderness, She is God. Glory be to She.

Life was good in the villages. There were great harvests of fish, grain, fruits and nuts. Hunting was excellent in the fertile valleys. The people prospered. The men toiled daily, fishing, planting, harvesting, hunting and building. The priestesses tended the temples singing praises to She and ministering to all the needs of the people.

One day a young man asked his male coworkers why they always were sent to work in the fields while the beautiful priestesses tended the temples. "We can sing and dance as well as they can," he said. "Why can't we spend our days and nights singing and dancing in the temples rather than sweating out here in the fields?"

The dark clouds of envy and suspicion gathered over the villages, and one day a group of male workers sullenly approached the sacred water temple and told the priestess that they too wished to sing and dance and tend the fires. The priestess explained to them that it would be impossible for males to tend the temples because the Water Goddess was She and She must be served by those who were born in her image. This answer infuriated the males who, being larger and stronger, bodily threw the priestesses out of the temple. They then announced to the village that from that day forward men would tend the temples.

The villagers laughed at their pretension and stopped going to that one temple. The male priests became so disturbed at this that they discarded their male garments and dressed themselves in the priestesses' robes. Daily, they performed what they could remember of the services they had seen. They practiced and pranced around in their beautiful robes singing and dancing. They faithfully tended the fires and replenished the basins with fresh water from the lake.

Eventually, a few of the villagers returned to the temple. Seeing this, other males seized other temples, dispossessing the priestesses and dressing themselves up in the long robes.

After many years, all the temples were served by males while the former priestesses busied themselves at cooking, sewing and other domestic tasks. As the ages passed, the priests decided that She was much too old and too tired to continue serving as God, so they called a major meeting and resolved that they would have a new God and it would be He. He is mighty, He is powerful, He is God, God the almighty. "Glory be to He," they sang as they danced around the temple fires in their beautiful long robes.

Meditation 3—Three Strange Events

With closed eyes, I entered the silence of the evening meditation. In the darkness, formless shadows merged with dancing, light streaks of soft, electric blue. Occasionally, random groups of vivid, tiny, blue dots of bright light peppered the darkness in front of me. Far to my left, a dim golden light beckoned and grew larger and larger. As it strengthened, it gradually evolved into a substance that soon became a very large birthday cake covered with candles.

The cake sat directly in front of me on a round table and the candles were brightly blazing. The decoration on the cake included a script that covered its sides, but I had no understanding of the words. I tried to count the candles but failed because there were too many. There must have been more than 150. Suddenly, dark shadows darted from both sides as an unknown force flipped the table, throwing the cake forward to fall upside down on the floor. The lights went out as the cake buried the candles beneath it. Then there was nothing.

After a short period of darkness, a pale green cloud drifted closer and closer. Soon I could see many books and stacks of papers in its center. There seemed to be box after box of books and papers piled everywhere. Hands with strong fingers appeared. They ripped the book covers off and tore the papers into shreds. Another box was broken open. The first book on top had the words *rebellio tumultus* printed in large type on its cover. The hands ripped it through the center and discarded the contents. This scene gradually faded into nothingness.

After a period of darkness, I suddenly realized I was looking at a brilliant, sunlit seashore. Out on the ocean, a sailing boat sped toward the land. It was a large boat with three tall masts and billowing red sails that strained in a brisk wind. At full speed, the boat was driven solidly onto the beach. Instantly, the crew swarmed up the rigging and cut all of the ropes with large knives. The red sails fluttered down to the deck where they were pushed over the side and down into the breaking waves on the sandy beach.

The crew then threw the ropes, cargo, furniture, bedding, and supplies overboard into the surf. When they were finished, all of them clambered down the sides of the boat and crossed the wide beach. Soon they vanished into the trees and dense foliage that lined the shore. The ship and all the details were very clear. There was a name on both the bow and the stern but someone had battered it with an axe so it could no longer be read. The light and the scene slowly faded away and I was again left in the silence and the darkness where I pondered on the meaning of these things.

Meditation 4—A Walk in Paradise

One very ancient meditation is called "A walk in paradise." It is thought to be the oldest formalized reflection known. It is a classic. This lesson was normally conducted by a spiritual leader who talked his students through the first part of the meditation and then left them in silence. The teacher's instructions were always given in story form.

Scholars tell us this meditation was used in ancient Persia 2,000 years ago. The inspiration to develop today's guided imagery techniques likely came from this historic source. The title, "A walk in paradise," may bring to current minds a vision of angels and cherubs surrounded by golden clouds; however, the original meaning and literal interpretation of the word "paradise" has a far more earthly connotation. The roots of the word come from both ancient Greece and Persia, and they indicate paradise as nothing more and nothing less than a protected, walled garden.

The Lost Paradise as described in the Bible was a closed Garden of Eden right here on earth. In ancient Persia, homes of the wealthy had an enclosed, garden courtyard complete with flowing water, lush greenery, and fruits and vegetables. The famous walled monastery gardens of the Middle Ages could be another example. The classic meditation, "A walk in paradise," went something like this:

Please imagine you are a student sitting in a dimly lit meditation room as your teacher addresses you:

"Relax your muscles and make yourself very comfortable. Relax and be comfortable; this is the first secret you must learn. Breathe slowly and regularly, and breathe deeply in a pleasant rhythm. I am going to tell you a story that will be helpful to you. You are now quite at ease. Nothing will disturb you during our time together.

"Did you know that you had a great secret? Well, you do. Somewhere there is a very private door and only you know the location. It could be at the far side of a special room, it could be underneath the stairway, or it may be hidden in a brick wall. You and you alone can see this particular door; it is invisible to all others. It is time for you to go to your secret door.

"Do not hesitate; you know where it is. Now is the time for you to use this door. Put out your hand and open the latch; now push the door open gently. It is perfectly safe and I will be with you. Step through the doorway so you can enter into the other side. Now, close the door behind you and fasten it with the lock. You are now in your own private paradise where no one can disturb you. This is your own sanctuary of peace, your own retreat, and it is always available to you by just stepping through your secret door.

"Look around and see the wonders of this beautiful garden. It is filled with shrubs, flowers, and tall trees swaying in the breeze. The sky is very, very blue with only two or three puffs of white fleecy clouds floating above to let your eyes see how rich the color of the sky can be. The sunlight is golden as it filters through the green leaves of the trees down to the carpet of flowers below. This is such a pleasing garden.

"Did you know that all of the plantings growing here are a result of beautiful thoughts from you? If you should see a weed at your feet, it would be nice to pull it out; it grew from a careless, negative thought. One good thought can pluck it out, roots and all, so always think good thoughts; it makes your pathway easier.

Look ahead of you down the meadows of your paradise for there are many. See the running brooks and hear the splash of a waterfall somewhere ahead. Walk forward and observe all the good things you have made possible. Wind your way around the shrubs and trees. Pause and see the countless varieties of tantalizing fruits and nuts that await should you become hungry.

"There is a small pond ahead where a cool waterfall splashes happily over the rocks down into the placid pool that is just the right size for swimming. Look closely and you will notice wisps of steam at the far end of the pond. They come from hot springs that bubble up from the depths of the earth. Here is a pond with hot water at one end and cold at the other. Exactly the right temperature for your pleasant bathing is waiting for you if you were to carefully choose the proper location to enter.

"The water from the pond flows into a nearby lake stocked with many fish and water plants. The sun shimmers on the tiny ripples that creep across the surface of the waters. The scintillating splashes of sunshine beckon you to come and enjoy this place.

"As you near the edge of the lake, you realize that anything you desire, whatever it may be, can be brought into your garden. However, this knowledge brings the burden of responsibility with it. You must be careful and choose your wishes wisely, for it is true that whatever you desire and put uppermost in your heart is likely to eventually occur. Do not be hasty in creating inflexible desires.

"A building is in the trees near the shore of the lake. Its style is one which you have always liked. It is a very good building and, as you approach it, you can observe everything about it very carefully. This building has many features that appeal to you, and you feel comfortable with it. It is good that you like it because this is the temple of your heart. It is yours and yours alone. Inside, there are many volumes you can study which will help you know yourself better. The temple is filled with things that are important to you and what you have been in the past. All are collected here in your temple. The many rooms and closets seem to be bursting; but, do not be dismayed, because there is room for much, much more. There will always be room here for more.

"You may enter your temple any time you choose. Enter now or wait until a later hour if you wish. There is no hurry in this garden. Enter your temple when you feel the time is right. That will be a good step forward.

"I must leave you now, for I shall visit my own temple for a short while. I leave you safely in your own paradise which is yours and yours alone. You know your own way in and out; you do not need me to ever come here with you again. I have the utmost confidence in you and your capabilities. As I leave, I must explain that you never need be lonely here because you can invite as many of your friends and loved ones to be with you as you wish. You can plan a picnic or a party. There are innumerable places here in paradise for those you truly love. Every choice is yours; everything is possible; this is your lesson, and I leave you now in the quiet. Farewell."

Mabel Dorland—Hypnotic Regression

I see a gold statue, an idol. It is raised quite high above a temple floor on a platform, covered with a fine, mesh-textured cloth of gold, that is caught in around the ankles. The idol has a very fine physique, very muscular, very much developed like an athlete. Though in a sitting position, it is not fat like a Buddha. It is a very beautiful person. There is a door in the solar plexus area, invisible underneath the rib cage until it opens. After the door opens to allow full view from in front and either side, a platform glides out. The crystal skull rests on this platform.

A woman enters dressed in beautiful shining silver, carrying two torches, one in each hand. Obviously she is a leader, in a high position. She wears around her head a band of silver with a deep, dark-red design on it. Her black hair is worn loose and free. Shoulder length in front, it hangs down her back, very loose and wavy.

The scene shifts to soldiers with thick, broad-bladed swords in mock battle on a field which is just outside the temple. This is a feast day of celebration for the crystal skull, which is not on view except on this one special day.

The crystal skull is now being removed from the idol and carried by two men in dark robes. One man follows in a gorgeous full-feather headdress which is reminiscent of the American Indian, but he is not an American Indian. The headdress is beautiful with thousands of feathers. He wears a loin cloth, but he is covered with intricate beadwork wherever he is not covered with feathers. The thousands of feathers are pure white, with a dark band toward the tip that means something important. His arms and legs are bare, and he wears a beaded arm bracelet above the elbow. He is a very big, powerful man, not dark skinned. His skin is creamy white, with lots of yellow and pink in it, not dark but not white.

He carries the crystal skull into a tunnel passageway made of enormous stones; it leads to a large, enclosed area with a central walkway lined on either side with seats and benches. The walkway is of a different colored stone, a golden beige. The area is large and completely enclosed or inside of a mountain. It is softly illuminated in a mysterious fashion. There is a door in the center of the floor. The door opens, and the crystal skull is handed down through the doorway to upstretched arms from below.

There is an oblong ceremonial chamber room below, also softly illuminated with no evidence of the light source. The skull is placed in the center of the room on a raised platform, where a special stand supports it. The stand is covered with a soft, non-reflective black material, not velvet but something similar. Only those charged with direct contact and care of the crystal skull can enter this submerged room, which is covered entirely with the black material.

No light can be seen except the crystal skull, which is brilliantly illuminated, shining like a star at midnight. The attendants also seem to be completely covered in black robes. Only their hands are visible; a hood covers much of the head and face. The hands of one attendant are cupped around the skull from both sides without touching it. These are my hands. I was one of the guardians of the skull.

I am left alone in the chamber with the skull for half of a day, 12 hours. Then I am replaced with another attendant. This cycle is repeated; the skull always has an attendant, for it is not known exactly when it might communicate. There must always be a supporting influence around it and it must never be left unguarded.

I am not touching it; it is between my hands. The jaw is moving very rapidly, as if in rapid speech. The skull seems to have hieroglyphs forming in the air out of its mouth. I am not manipulating the skull, it is acting of its own accord.

It says: "From eons of time peace has been sought by the Brotherhood, and many more eons will pass before that peace is achieved, for man is still too blind to see. He strives, vainly, without reason. The light is still too strong; he would be blinded by its brilliance. Do not despair, for though the time may seem to go slowly, it is but a breath. I come to you now to bring a blessing for all who wish to strive for deeper understanding. For all those who strive will find peace. The sapphire shall remain near me."

The sapphire sits to the left of the crystal skull. It is a deep blue in color around the edge, becoming lighter blue on the crown—a carved stone, highly polished, bound with a single band of silver around the bottom.

The crystal skull speaks again: "There are many more things I can tell you if you return to this room again with me. I beg you, have no fear, as I am of the light."

And another time: "The ways of men are very small compared to the vastness of the universe. Surely as the stars shine, there is a vast, inner, connecting web that runs between the universe and this planet. There are few who can see. As time goes on, there will be more and more who will become enlightened. Do not forget the sapphire. It sits always to my left."

Mabel Dorland—Meditation

Three men appear, dressed in typical Arabian costumes of hundreds of years ago. They say they know of the crystal skull; they had worked with it. It was once in a fortress citadel, high in the mountains. Built of granite, the citadel sat on solid rock, almost black in color. Within the citadel was a circular room covered by a circular dome. The skull sat on a raised pedestal in the room's center. A high window was placed in the dome far above and behind, constructed in such a way that sunlight hit a diagonal shaft coming down from the ceiling, which in turn focused on the rear of the skull, illuminating the face. This gave the appearance of a very bright light in front of the skull. Another hole in the ceiling permitted the moonlight to enter on certain full moons and create the same effect.

Frank Dorland—Hypnotic Regression

On an extremely high mountain, with ridges of mountains as far as the eye can see, I am on my way to a secret chamber. There is a passageway which, if I follow carefully, I can keep going—just when it seems there is no other place to go, there is always a little turn, a place to inch upward through a crevice. I have done this many times. I see below a large cave with a small stream in it.

There is a large entrance where animals and birds go in and out, but I use this higher, secret entrance. I am one of the Secret Brotherhood. I have a load of clay on my back, for it is my task to dig it out of the river bank, a day's journey below me in the valley. There are cities on the river, but we could not keep our work secret there.

I make this trip alone, prepared by many prayers. I have only one weapon, a leather sling that has a large stone in it. When I swing it around my head, I can trip a place in the leather sack that lets the stone out. The stone can go about 20 feet before it is stopped by the leather thong tied around it. This is a particular type of stone that always finds its mark and it is important that I save it. It has a hole in it so that, when I swing it around my head, it makes a screaming noise. This sound scares anyone away and I seldom have to defend myself.

The passageway I am in is really a cleft, an almost invisible stairway with little stones jutting out for hand- and footholds. I come to a space where two rocks are forced together in a crevice and there is just room for me to squeeze through. Inside, I am in a dark tunnel, quite round and polished, which I follow a short way until I come to a place where it has caved in. Below me on the floor of the cave I see large animals, similar to wolves, and a funny type of bear. The Brotherhood labored long to make a walkway to connect to the next part of the tunnel. It is wood and plastered over with mud to hide it from sight from the cave below.

There are many rooms off the main tunnel. I only know of the major room where we eat, the workroom and the room I share with four other men. There are no women in this area; it is an all-male brotherhood, secret from the women and from the cities. We have our representatives in the major cities, who are priests.

We are making the crystal skull. We are also making the divining stars for the brotherhood to use. I have a work area where I take the wet clay and spread it out. There are flat rocks at the stovetop. The clay dries hard and fast, like large pieces of flat bread. I then rake it up, crumble it, pound it into fine pieces and mix it with the fat of birds we catch.

We catch birds to eat. We cook the bones and the rest of the bird to make a broth. The fat comes to the top, is skimmed off and mixed with the dried clay that has been ground to dust. This makes a waterproof clay. It is used to surround the skull to hold it so that we can work on it. I have a large amount of clay that I am working and a large amount that is finished and ready.

The main room is large, big enough to hold 45 or 50 people comfortably. The skull is at one end near a crevice that drips water from a fault in the rock. The water is collected in a large chamber hollowed out of the rock. It holds a great amount of water, which we use constantly in working on the skull. The skull sits upon a flat rock surrounded by the water-proofed clay. Only a tiny part of it is exposed, the portion we are working on.

We mix a poultice of water and sand obtained from the floor of the cave. A rock about the size of a flattened orange is rubbed back and forth across the crystal, and the sand wears the crystal away to shape it. A soft, dirty powder comes off, which we carefully save. It is used to eliminate all the scratches. All the ground-up crystal and sand is saved and used over and over until it grinds so fine that the skull is polished. It takes a lot of patience, but that is what we are here for. We are living in this cave to make the skull.

We also make small skulls, small enough to hold in the palm of the hand. They are also worn around the neck on a piece of leather, but generally are kept hidden in a bag out of sight.

The air in the room is always clean and fresh. There are many clefts in the long, smooth tunnel and rocks where the air comes through and goes up into cracks at the other end of the tunnel somewhere in the mountain. The water always comes through this one cracked area, never varying, always cool, never hot nor cold. We do all the cooking in another room. The smoke goes up and disappears. The long passageway, that is round like a tube, goes into many other passageways until it gets so small we cannot go any further. The passageway continues, but we do not know where it goes or how it was formed.

Again in regression, I asked to see how the crystal skull was made. I was taken to a place in the mountains, almost to the timberline. Above, higher, there was snow.

I was told, "Here is where the cities get their power."

I was shown three buildings in a row. They were shaped, on one side like the seats in an amphitheater, in a rounded horseshoe shape. All three buildings were connected with a passageway, completely enclosed. There were nine stories in each building. The curved portion faced south, and it curved so that, when the sun rose, it would shine on one side; as it moved, throughout the day, it would be facing a part of the curved area.

The back side of the building was flat and was sealed; there were windows only on the side that was curved. The windows were all sealed. They appeared to be glass.

On the back side, there was an enormous ball behind each building. In the front of each building, there was a long pole, similar to a flagpole, about four feet in diameter, in the center of the area that faced the curved portion. I was told that, as the sun would swing all day long, there were reflectors in the curve of the building that reflected and focused the sun onto this long shaft, which was straight up and down.

It was explained that the sunlight, by being focused on this, did something to the crystals in the vertical shaft. The shaft went down into a tunnel underneath the ground where it turned and passed completely underneath the building, coming up out of the ground in back. It ended in a connection with the large ball, which was constantly being filled with some kind of energized material that circulated between it and the shaft in front. The building was sealed because it was dangerous to be either in front of it or in back.

A great many people worked in these buildings. I was taken inside and shown the ground floor. On the first three floors, men were allowed, because men did the heavy work. Above the third floor, no man was allowed; only females worked from the fourth to the ninth floors. All had technical jobs, adjusting mirrors and whatever it was that put the sunlight, and the energy from the sunlight, onto this shaft which contained the crystals.

It was further explained that it was not the visible part of the light that had anything to do with the energy. The visible part of the light only enabled them to use that as a guide to focus the energy onto this vertical shaft. I was not allowed on the other floors because I was a man, and I was not told how this worked, other than that there was a difference between the back side of the building and the front side. It was this difference between the two that was the source of the energy.

No one was allowed or dared to go out in the back. They said that was the area of Hell. Heaven was the area in front. If you went out into Heaven, you would be burned. If you went out into Hell,

you also would be burned. You had to stay in the building. I was led
to believe it had something to do with an energy that was radioactive. It was extremely dangerous to go outside of the building.

There was a long passageway by which to enter these buildings. It went beyond a hill, so that you had to enter from down
below, over the hill. You went through the hill and came out into a
passageway that went into the three buildings, all of which were
connected by the enclosed passageways.

On the bottom three floors, there was a manufacturing process. There was a regular railway, and something about the size of
grains of rice, a light tan in color, was being put into little cars and
taken to the end building. There, the grain-like material was sealed
into little packages, then taken down to the cities.

It was explained to me that these little packages of granules
could be put into a regenerative box, and the box would, in turn,
generate the power and energy to run a city. It did not need to be a
central distribution system. Each home, each business, each block
had these rejuvenating boxes in which so many packages of granules were put, and that gave the energy needed.

This was some type of solar energy from a reflector onto crystals that received the sunlight and in turn affected whatever it was
that went underground to the storage tank in the back.

I asked repeatedly to be shown how the crystal skull was
made. I was taken to a city in an area of sunshine and palm trees. I
walked up the main street to an enormous building. This was a
library, where the main priests lived, a secret brotherhood of a different era. The library had volume after volume of books much as
our own, yet this city existed many thousands of years ago.

I was taken upstairs; there must have been at least six floors to
the building. The top area was where the brotherhood would reju-
venate themselves in a type of clinic. They had a way to take away
years of deterioration from the physical body.

The roof was flat, like a football field. It had a very decorative
railing around it, pierced so that air could pass through. It was very
brilliant on the roof. On one end, there was a pool of water, raised
about three feet above the roof, like a large swimming pool. The
side of the pool of water that faced toward where people could sit
was curved like the seats in an amphitheater. There were reflectors

of abalone shells, cut into round shapes and set a few inches apart. These were behind the curved area, behind the water, but in a curved position so that, no matter where the sun was, its light reflected from these reflectors to a position in the center of this pool of water.

Center and front, like the front seat in the orchestra, the crystal skull sat on a platform, above the water about two feet. Seated in the area and facing the water, we were about eye level with the skull. The skull sat there in the blazing sun above the water, with the sunlight reflecting on it. It was a very brilliant thing to see.

There were many people sitting in chairs, looking at the skull. They were silent, in meditation. They were wrapped in white cloths like a sheet, which went over their heads and over their faces, so that only a slit opened for the eyes. It was very bright, very hot.

At one-minute intervals, a young girl came up with a crystal pitcher or crystal ladle. She would ladle up about a pint of water from the pool and pour it on top of the crystal skull. When she poured the water on the skull, because of the brilliance of the light hitting it, the water seemed to burst into thousands of tiny stars that almost exploded. They scintillated, danced, jumped in the air, like thousands of energetic molecules going in all directions.

Just as this quieted down, another girl would come, and the process was repeated. We were just sitting there, watching in meditation. It was explained to me that this rejuvenated the bodies, minds and spirits. Only the ruling brotherhood, the ones who were ruling this kingdom, received this.

The common people had a very different type of life. They were kept in ignorance, without knowledge, to do the menial work.

CARE OF CRYSTALS

Volumes have been written about keeping crystals in safe and secret places. "It must be kept in a black velvet bag securely tied with a braided purple ribbon," states one expert. "Never," says another, "the crystal must always be carefully wrapped three times, in the finest black, raw silk and kept in a dark place so it cannot pick up any evil influences."

"They are all wrong as can be," another states. "The best way to keep a crystal safe and undefiled is to get a blue china bowl and fill it to the brim with the purest of sea salt. Bury the crystal deep in the salt and it will remain there, clean and pure, ready to be used again. The salt protection is better if a pure white beeswax candle is kept next to the blue china bowl."

So these opinions are each important to the ones who put faith in formulas of this nature. I believe the main requirement in keeping a crystal is selecting a place that would be neat, clean, safe and convenient. Since a crystal is a valuable tool, it should be treated as such. A velvet bag, a leather pouch, or even a small cardboard box should serve very well.

There are a few warnings. Obviously, a crystal should not be left on a window sill where the rays of the sun might concentrate through it and start a fire. Neither should a crystal be placed in a dresser drawer along with certain cosmetic tools such as emery boards or nail files. While real quartz crystal cannot be scratched by the hardest steel machinist's file, most modern nail files have a surface of synthetic diamonds or emery dust which is sure to scratch the surface of any crystal or anything else.

One safekeeping practice apparently rewards its users, and that is the custom of wrapping the crystal in selected colored cloths to give certain added powers as needed. As an example, if one were to wish for a more harmonious and tranquil life, that individual's personal crystal could be wrapped in a blue cloth while it was not being used, because blue has the color vibration of peace and harmony. For added effectiveness, the desire for peace should also be verbally programmed aloud into the crystal as it is being wrapped in the blue cloth. Natural material such as cotton or silk is believed to be preferable to a synthetic fiber. The idea is to surround the crystal at rest with the particular color vibration chosen for a specific task. This vibration is then thought to be available from the crystal when needed. Color psychology is used to good advantage.

A well-known western U.S. attorney keeps a hand crystal by his private desk telephone, masqueraded as a paperweight. His decision (meditation) crystal is in his top desk drawer wrapped in an ancient green silk handkerchief. These are tools of his trade; his successes are due to his mental victories. The green handkerchief is a lucky piece, but the crystal actually responds to his energies.

Conclusion

In this book I have related tales of the thoughts, beliefs, practices, facts and fancies of the people of many races about their crystals. Some of this material dates back far beyond the days of ancient Babylon.

Our modern records disclose that solid-state electronics have been in use only since 1948, but we must keep in mind that thousands of wonderworkers have relied on a piece of quartz crystal as their own personal solid state device for at least 12,000 years if not longer.

Our ancient forefathers left us a tangible lesson in the shape of a human skull. A skull carved out of a solid chunk of clear rock crystal which in itself is everlasting because crystal does not age or decay. Their message declares that the human mind is the most important asset in this universe. The skull is of course a magnificently engineered protective container to hold this treasure. The human skull is truly marvelous, but it's what is inside that really counts.

We are now living in this new Age of Communications. Most people call it the Age of Aquarius, which astrologers say started in the 1880s, and is reputed to take about 300 years to get in full swing. If we could count up our advancements since 1880, we would soon realize that there have been more achievements in this short span than the entire sum total of improvements gained over the last 12,000 years. This is the most fascinating time to be alive in the whole history of mankind.

Perhaps the crystal skull surfaced at this time as a harbinger of a new and better age. If that is true, perhaps this spinning globe carrying its cargo of humanity is far more than an astral accident in space as some believe. We could postulate that crystal is designed to play a major role for some distant tomorrow. The earth's crust is abundantly supplied with silicon dioxide in the form of quartz crystals liberally peppered throughout.

Electronic engineers have explained that a crystal-studded planet would broadcast a constant stream of radio signals. Such a signal beam could serve as a navigational beacon for celestial journeys. Could it be that our world spinning through this relatively isolated place in space has a divine, predestined purpose?

Our earth scientists have said that the world is slowly getting closer and closer to the sun. Sometime in the far future this planet will become too heated to sustain any life. The only salvation for the human race would be to move out of the old world to a new world of tomorrow waiting out there somewhere in space. An unfailing navigational signal beam from the earth would be a great safety factor for mass shuttle travel to another planet.

If all of this proves true, is it not strange that both the past and future of mankind is so intertwined with electronic quartz crystals? From the very beginning when they were thought to be Holy Ice to our current understanding of them as nature's solid state transducers, the electronic crystal has inspired, assisted and guided countless thousands of fertile minds toward solving problems and striving for better and better tomorrows.

The Spiral Stairway

The spiral stairway glistens
Beneath our feet.
It windingly descends below
Into the dim lost past
From whence we came.

We shall ascend each rise
That lies before us.
There is no turning back
Upon these crystal steps of life.

It matters not
How many years it takes
To reach each goal that beckons.
Giant strides to cut the time
Is worthless contemplation.

Together, let us climb
These crystal heights before us.
The constant light above
Illuminates our way.

One shining golden day
We shall rise above the stars themselves
And find the other side
Where dwell the Gods
And all of their creations.
                    —Frank Dorland, 1978

Note: The spiral stairway refers to the spiral cell growth of a perfect quartz crystal and to the energies of the mind and the universe that are projected outward in ever-widening spirals.

Glossary

Amethyst: Pale to purple or dark violet. Color caused by irradiation. Heat treatment may remove color or may turn amethyst to deep red-yellow or pale green.

Amplifier: A device that puts out an enlarged reproduction of the essential features of the input. An electron tube, a transistor, a magnetic circuit. In metaphysics, an electronic working crystal.

Amplifying Reflector: An electronic quartz crystal with rounded and polished surfaces to receive, amplify and broadcast energies.

Angel's Hair: Rutilated crystal. Clear crystal with long, hair-like strands of titanium dioxide included. It looks like baby hair and may be in color shades from silver to blonde to golden yellow. Occasionally darker shades.

Antenna: That portion of a receiving station or receiver designed to collect and receive radiating waves of energy from space. In commerce, an antenna is usually made from metal wires or rods. Dish antennas reflect the radio energy entering the system. In metaphysics, the human body with its high moisture content balanced with electrolytes is believed to be a superb receiving antenna.

Apport: Apportation, teleportation. The mysterious conveyance of material objects into a closed or sealed room. Writings, symbols, pictures mysteriously appearing. Objects such as coins, medals, books, flowers, live lobsters, live animals or birds materializing in front of a medium and/or audience.

Autoclave: A heavy container for high-pressure chemical reactions.

Catoptromancy: Divination by means of mirrors.

Citrine: Pale champagne to deep yellow quartz crystal. Sometimes "topaz" color. Frequently sold as topaz.

Cristobalite: A white, chalky material used in refractory linings. It is a form of quartz crystal, which changes into cristobalite at 1470 degrees centigrade.

Cryptocrystalline Quartz: Quartz in granular to fibrous aggregate forms. Common varieties are: chalcedony, carnelian, chrysophrase, chrysocolla, agates, jasper, onyx, flint and chert. Opal is similar to chalcedony but contains 4% to 9% water.

Crystal: Means clear or transparent. A three-dimensional atomic structure in which the atoms have geometric regularity and are precisely repeated throughout the structure. In common use, glass is substituted for crystal; i.e., set the table with silver and crystal now means to set the table with glassware and stainless steel. Common glassware. A protective cover for watch faces.

Crystal Ball: Originally a globe carved out of rock crystal. In common use today to describe a glass globe supposedly useful for scrying. Over 98 per cent of modern crystal balls are glass, lead crystal (glass) or plastic.

Crystal Control: Control of the frequency of an oscillator by utilizing a specially designed and cut electronic crystal.

Crystal Controlled Transmitter: A radio or TV transmitter in which broadcast frequencies are directly controlled by a crystal oscillator.

Crystal Operation: A functioning circuit using crystal controlled oscillators.

Crystal Set: A simple radio receiver consisting of a galena crystal (a crystalline form of lead sulfide) for demodulation of the received signal and no amplifier stage. The sound was usually reproduced through an electronic crystal headset in which the mechanical displacement was caused by the quartz crystal's piezo-electric action. The quartz crystal served as a transducer which turned electrical signals into sound.

Damping: Reduction of energy by absorption or radiation. The process of reducing and controlling the amplitude of oscillations.

Electronic Crystal: A high-quality single quartz crystal in which the constituent atoms are arranged in geometric regularity and are precisely repeated. A piezoelectric crystal.

Fused Quartz: Quartz which has been heated into a molten state and then allowed to cool. It no longer retains any crystalline structure.

Hydrothermal Transport Growth: A method of refining natural quartz crystal into electronic quartz crystal.

Iolite: Also known as cordierite. Often found in Finland and Norway. A transparent gem of pale to deep violet color. The gem changes color from violet to straw yellow depending on whether it is viewed through north light or south light. Sometimes called the Vikings' navigation crystal.

Lead Crystal: A soft, lustrous fusible glass with a high lead oxide content. Also known as flint glass.

Meditation: A devotional exercise of the mind. Mental contemplation. A state of mind in which the consciousness is expanded and developed. Also mental control for complete relaxation and emptying of the mind.

Milky Quartz: Snow quartz. Rock crystal filled with numerous liquid and gas inclusions. Looks whitish like snow or milk. Best qualities are beautiful, snow white. Not electronic because of impurities.

Oscillator: An electronic device that generates alternating-current power controlled by a piezoelectric crystal.

Piezoelectricity: The generation of electrical polarity or electricity in a dielectric crystal when subjected to pressure or mechanical stress; also the generation of stress in a crystal when voltage is applied such as in a crystal oscillator.

Pleochroism: The characteristic of some crystals to show different colors when seen along different axes.

Quartz: The tektosilicate family of minerals commonly divided into two divisions: crystalline quartz and cryptocrystalline quartz. The crystals are hexagonal and grow both left handed and right handed. The granular form is tough but brittle such as flint.

Quartz Crystal: Known as crystalline quartz. The species includes rock crystal, smoky quartz, amethyst, citrine, rose quartz, blue quartz and quartz with inclusions such as rutilated, tourmalinated, aventurine, tiger eye and others.

Quartz Crystal, Refined: The highest quality electronic crystal. The refining process is accomplished in large autoclaves. Small pieces of quartz crystal called feed stock are dissolved in mineralized water subjected to heat and pressure. Impurities are left behind on the bottom of the container as the individual cells of the dissolved crystals migrate. The cells attach themselves to seed crystals suspended in the upper region. Large blocks of crystal are grown in a few weeks' time. These refined pure crystal blocks are the preferred choice of electronic engineers. Many jewelers and lapidary shops erroneously label the refined crystals as synthetic.

Receiver: A device equipped for reception of incoming electrically transmitted signals. In metaphysics, the human body.

Reflector: A reflector element of one or more conducting surfaces for reflecting energy. Specifically, an electronic quartz crystal.

Reproducer: A device such as a speaker or headphones that translates electrical symbols into sound waves. In a television receiver the reproducer includes the picture as well as sound. In metaphysics, the brain translates incoming pulses of energy into pictures, sounds, odors, taste sensations and touch.

Rock Crystal: High quality transparent crystalline quartz.

Rutilated Quartz: Rock crystal with inclusions of rutile, a crystalline form of titanium dioxide.

Scrying: Divination by gazing into a crystal ball, "shewstone," magic mirror or bowl of liquid.

Silver: A lustrous, white malleable metal. Has the highest thermal and electrical conductivity of all metals. Widely used in electrical contacts and printed circuit boards. Historically silver is a spiritual metal designated for religious usage. Silver is the metal symbol of the moon. One of the fabulous four religious elements—

crystal, water, silver, and the moon.

Smoky Quartz: Quartz crystal that may range in color from pale brown to almost black. Color may be warm or cold. Color due to irradiation.

Solid State: Pertains to electronic circuits and components using semi-conductors. Solid state materials are transistors, diodes, semiconductors, transducers, etc.

Telepathy: Communication through the exercise of mental projection. Communication through mental exercises during meditation or times of stress. Communication via mystical powers.

Transducer: A device such as piezoelectric crystal that converts energy input of one form into output energy of another. Electronic crystal.

Transistor: An active semiconductor made of silicon having three or more electrodes: the emitter, base and collector.

Tridymite: A form of quartz with small, twinned crystals found in igneous rock. Quartz crystal changes into this form at 867 degrees centigrade.

Tuner: A circuit that can be selectively tuned to any desired frequency of broadcast wavelengths. In metaphysics, the human mind acts as the tuner to select the desired reception.

Wavelength: The distance between points of a corresponding phase of two consecutive cycles of a rising and falling electromagnetic wave. Wavelengths travel at approximately the speed of light.

Working Crystal: Any high quality electronic quartz crystal carved and polished for use in meditation, dream control, metaphysical usage, mind control, or other mental exercises such as heightening the intuition, creative endeavors, healing purposes, etc. For best results, the crystal would have rounded and polished surfaces to facilitate the broadcasting of energies fed into the crystal by the user. A good working crystal can be of clear rock crystal, smoky, citrine, blue, rose, amethyst, green, etc. The color does not matter so much as the electronic transmission facilities of the electronic crystal.

Working Crystal Ball: A globe carved out of high quality electronic crystal. It may be clear or colored. The globe may be optically ground and polished, or it may be hand carved and irregular or a bit lopsided. Irregular balls do not need a special stand. They don't roll away.

Working Handpiece: A high quality electronic crystal carved to fit comfortably in the hand. A working handpiece has gently rounded surfaces and often has finger grooves. One end may be broad and one end may be rather small if the handpiece was designed for acupressure use.

Working Pendant: A high quality crystal designed and carved to be suspended and worn. The design may be a simple oval, triangle, or circle like a full moon. Other popular shapes are crosses, ankhs, eternal circle rings, crescent moons, hearts, shields, etc.

Bibliography

American Geological Institute. *Dictionary of Geological Terms.* New York: Doubleday, 1980.

Anderson, B.S. *Gem Testing.* New York: Emerson Books, 1948.

Baigent, Michael, Richard Leigh, and Henry Lincoln. *Holy Blood, Holy Grail.* New York: Dell Publishing Co., Inc., 1983.

Barber, R.W. *Arthur of Albion.* Great Britain: Barrie & Rockliff, 1961.

Bessy, Maurice. *Magic & the Supernatural.* Spring Books, 1968.

Blavatsky, H. P. *The Secret Doctrine.* 2 vols. London: The Theosophical Publishing Company, Limited, 1888.

Boyd, Robert. *Tells, Tombs and Treasures.* New York: Bonanza Books, 1979.

Budge, Wallace. *Amulets and Talismans.* University Books, 1960.

Campbell, Joseph. *The Masks of God.* 4 vols. Viking Press, 1970

Campbell, Joseph, and Eisler Gimbutas: *Muses: In All Her Names.* San Francisco: Harper, 1991.

Canaday, John & Katherine. *Keys to Art.* France: Tudor Publications, 1962.

Cavendish, Richard. *Man, Myth & Magic.* 24 vols. Italy: B.P.C., Publ., 1970.

Churchward, James. *The Lost Continent of Mu.* London: Neville Spearman Ltd., 1959.

Crow, W. B. *Precious Stones.* London: Aquarian Press, 1969.

Daraul, Arkon. *History of Secret Societies.* New York: Citadel Press, 1968.

De Givry, Grillot. *Witchcraft, Magic & Alchemy.* New York: Dover, 1971.

Desautels ,Paul E. *The Gem Kingdom.* New York: Random House, no date.

Evans, Joan. *Magical Jewels.* Oxford University Press, 1922.

Gimbutas, Jarija. *The Language of the Goddess.* Harper, 1989.

Goldberg. *The Sacred Fire.* University Books, 1958.

Hall, Manly P. *The Secret Teachings of All Ages.* Philosophical Research, 1972.

Hawkins, Gerald. *Stonehenge Decoded.* New York: Dell Books, 1966.

Hodges, Henry. *Artifacts.* London: Baker Publishing, 1964.

Holms, Al Campbell. *Facts of Psychic Science.* University Books, 1969.

International Council of Scholars. *Encyclopedia of World Art.* 15 vols. Rome: McGraw Hill, 1968.

Instituto Geografico De Agostini. *World of Minerals.* Milan, 1971.

Kardec, Allan. *Book of Mediums.* New York: Samuel Weiser, 1970.

Kaster, Joseph. *Putnam's Mythological Dictionary.* New York: Putnam, 1963.

Kurz, Otto. *Fakes.* New York: Dover, 1967.

LaRousse Encyclopedia of Mythology. Hamlyn Publishing, 1968.

Long, Max Freedom. *Secret Science at Work.* DeVorss & Co., 1953.

Loomis, R. S. *Arthurian Literature in the Middle Ages.* Oxford Univ., 1959

Mair, Rosyln. *Key Dates in Art History.* Oxford: Pahidon, 1979.

Massignon, G. *Folk Tales of France.* University of Chicago Press, 1968.

Melville, John. *Crystal Gazing.* Weiser Books, 1970.

Metraux, Alfred. *History of the Incas.* New York: Schocken Books, 1970.

Monaghan, Patricia. *Goddesses & Heroines.* St. Paul, MN: Llewellyn Publications, 1990.

Munro, Eleanor C. *Encyclopedia of Art.* New York: Golden Press. 1977.

Nassau, Kurt. *Gems Made By Man.* Chilton Books, 1980.

Nuttall, Zelia. *Codex Nuttall.* New York: Dover, 1975.

O'Donoghue, Michael. *Quartz.* London: Butterworths, 1987.

Ostrander & Schroeder. *Psychic Discoveries Behind the Iron Curtain.* Prentice Hall, 1970.

Sinkankas, John. *Mineralogy.* New York: Van Nostrand Reinhold, 1964.

Sinkankas & Boegel. *Studio Handbook of Minerals.* New York: Viking Press, 1972.

Shubnikov & Sheftal. *Growth of Crystals.* London: Chapman & Hall, 1959.

Spence, Lewis. *Encyclopedia of Occultism.* University Books, 1960.

Tedlock, Dennis. *Popol Vuh.* Simon & Schuster, 1985.

Valiant, George. *The Aztecs of Mexico.* Doubleday Books, 1944.

Von Hagen, Victor. *The Desert Kingdom of Peru.* Mentor Books, 1968.

Numerous conversations with visiting dignitaries and scholars

Numerous library references

Dorland Working Crystals

Dorland working crystals have been in demand since 1968 when pioneer biocrystallographer Frank Dorland first made them available. He personally hand carved the crystals to supply requests from Australia, Bavaria, Italy, Spain, France, England and Canada as well as the United States.

In 1989, he found he could no longer supply the crystals, primarily because of the demands on his time for research, teaching and writing. He began looking for students to carry on his carving technique. He found Tom Struble, a natural and talented crystal carver whose work was true to purpose, style and quality.

Dorland Crystals are now available through Dorland's star student, Tom Struble. For complete information on Dorland Crystals, colors, sizes, styles and prices, send SASE to:

Holy Ice
c/o Tom Struble
Crystal Creations
PO Box 6003
Los Osos, CA 93412

THE LOST PYRAMIDS OF ROCK LAKE
BY FRANK JOSEPH

Was Atlantis in Wisconsin? Now, for the first time, here is proof of ancient, sacred pyramids at the bottom of a small lake in Wisconsin! Learn about the fascinating secrets of a great people who erected structures on land and in water as sophisticated astronomical observatories for their bloody sky cult.

This lake is 40 miles west of Milwaukee, Wisconsin. In 1989 author Frank Joseph organized the first side-scan sonar sweep of Rock Lake for the elusive structures. His instruments revealed an unprecedented panorama on the lake floor by way of images transposed from sound waves. The high-tech method identified a colossal stone mound shaped like an elongated pyramid 60 feet below the surface, and his research subsequently received widespread attention in the regional press.

Joseph has traveled the world over for revealing clues to the lost history of prehistoric Wisconsin, and is presently working with state authorities to have Rock Lake declared an official historic site. Trace the development of this ancient culture and read about amazing parallels with similar prehistoric cultures in the Canary Islands.

1-880090-04-X, 6 x 9, 208 pgs., illus., color plates, softcover $10.95

JOURNEYS: The Adventures of Leaf
BY LOUANN CARROLL

Journeys is a delightful story for young and old readers alike. It is the tale of a distressed maple leaf whose tenuous hold on the tree is broken by the cool, fall wind. His many adventures teach him much about life and friendship. He believes his life is over, but when we read about a new bud on the same tree in the following springtime, we know the spirit of Leaf has been reborn in a new form.

Included are delightful drawings from a seventh-grade art class who had listened to the story, demonstrating the impact the story's values had on the insightful students. These drawings are suitable for coloring in a variety of mediums.

Although this is a children's story, each person who reads *Journeys* interprets it differently. To the author it means:

"Life is full of journeys. Some roads you choose are more difficult than others. Though some people would believe you are wrong in your choosing, each person is guided by their inner being to that choice which is right for them. You must not feel guilty that your choice sometimes differs from what is thought best by those who love you. You must live your life, then die, only to live again."

1-880090-03-1, 10 x 7, 40 pgs., illus., softcover $9.95

HUMOR TRAVELS WELL
BY PETE DOCHERTY

A funny story can happen anywhere, and here is a book that proves it. Written by Peter Docherty, the president of a travel incentive business in Edina, Minnesota, **Humor Travels Well** is a collection of 22 heartwarming and hilarious stories taken from the author's experiences as a travel professional.

With this book, you'll travel with Pete to places and situations beyond imagination—to lunching with nobility, being detained at a Soviet airport and attending a third-rate English theatre (where you'll witness theatrics with a drama all their own). You'll discover how Pete learned the subtleties of Brazilian sign language, how he summoned up enough politeness to eat a sheep's eyeball, and how he managed to keep his cool as an honored guest at a human cremation.

But best of all, the stories in **Humor Travels Well** will introduce you to unforgettable people from around the world. You'll meet celebrities and royalty from many nations, serious as well as drunken officials, snake charmers and maharajahs, students of many specialities—from medicine to American slang—not to mention the American travelers for whom Pete has served as a guide.

And you'll find that humor is truly the universal language—from Beijing to Barbados, Rome to Rio, the Soviet Union to Scandinavia. Let Pete Docherty be your guide to adventures of all kinds across the globe. We guarantee that you won't need a translator!

0-880090-007, 5-1/4 x 8, 192 pgs., illus., softcover **$5.95**

To order books, please send full amount plus $1.50 for postage and handling for orders under $10.00, $3.00 for orders over $10.00.

Send orders to:

GALDE PRESS, INC.
P.O. Box 65611-89
St. Paul, Minnesota 55165